Parties
and Pressure Groups

Second Edition

W. N. Coxall

Longman
London and New York

British Library Cataloguing in Publication Data

Coxall, W. N.
   Parties and pressure groups. — 2nd ed. —
   (Political realities)
   1. Pressure groups — Great Britain
   I. Title   II. Series
   322.4'3'0941   JN329.P7

   ISBN 0-582-35189-8

Library of Congress Cataloguing in Publication Data

Coxall, W. N.
   Parties and pressure groups.

   (Political realities)
   Includes index.
   Summary: Examines the structure of the British
   political system and the role of the major and
   minor parties and pressure groups.
   1. Political parties — Great Britain. 2. Pressure
   groups — Great Britain. [1. Political parties —
   Great Britain. 2. Pressure groups — Great Britain.
   3. Great Britain — Politics and government] I. Title.
   II. Series.

   JN1121.C685 1985   324.241   85-11637
   ISBN 0-582-35189-8

Contents

Preface to the second edition

Whilst the aims and general framework of this book remain unaltered from the first edition, the extensive developments in British politics since the late 1970s have made necessary substantial changes in content. New case-studies begin chapter 1(on the 1983 general election) and chapter 5(on the Campaign for Nuclear Disarmament and the miners' strike of 1984–5). Chapter 2 has been considerably revised to take into account contemporary trends in electoral and parliamentary politics and chapter 7 contains additional material on trade union ballots. Chapter 3 has been substantially re-written to encompass changes in the policies of the two major parties, in the formation and activities of their internal groupings and in the constitution and leadership of the Labour Party. In addition to up-dated sections on the Liberal and nationalist parties, chapter 4 contains new sections on the Social Democratic Party and the Ecology Party and the discussions of the National Front, the Communist Party of Great Britain and the Ulster Unionist Council have been updated and expanded into broader considerations of the extreme right, the extreme left and the Northern Ireland parties respectively. Finally, major changes have been made in chapter 6 in order to examine the overall consequences for the party and pressure group system of the period of Conservative Government after 1979.

Once again, I should like to record my thanks to the general editor of the series, Derek Heater on this occasion for his valuable suggestions on the revised draft.

W. N. C.

1 Parties and Pressure groups in British Politics

The 1983 general election

On Thursday 9 June 1983, British voters went to the polls in a general election. As usual, they were faced with a wide range of issues on which to make up their minds including defence, law and order, unemployment, inflation and the future of the welfare state. Underlying them all, however, was a more basic decision: did electors want to confirm the Conservative Government in power for a further term of office, or was it time for a change? If it was, the question was more complex than simply putting the Labour opposition back into power. On this occasion, a third grouping – the Social Democratic Party–Liberal Alliance – had entered the field nationwide with some prospect of success. But in any case, the decision boiled down to one about parties and their credibility. Although unable to campaign directly, pressure groups also were active during the election, lobbying the parties and working on their behalf. The election campaign, therefore, forms a good point at which to begin a book on parties and pressure groups.

Parties must take election campaigns very seriously indeed. This is the case even though they know that the party which enters the campaign with a reasonable lead is unlikely to lose it during the campaign. Although considerable numbers of voters decide how to vote *during* the campaign, it is far from clear how many of them make the decisions they do *as a result* of the campaign. For example, in October 1974, the Labour Party began with a respectable lead in the opinion polls and held this lead throughout the campaign; in 1979, the sizeable Conservative advantage at the outset had diminished only slightly by polling day. But parties dare not appear complacent: not to be seen to be trying is a certain way of giving the game to their opponents.

Anyway, the capture of floating voters in marginal constituencies *can* make a crucial difference to the result and parties must therefore work hard to do this. All the time, moreover, the thought of the grave consequences elections can have will serve to intensify the parties' efforts. The 1979 election, for example, broke the Labour Government, abruptly terminating scores of ministerial careers. At the same time it gave Britain its first female Prime Minister, and began or renewed the governing roles of as many leading Conservatives. It cast down James Callaghan, not only ending his premiership but also helping to bring his leadership of the Labour Party to a premature conclusion. It raised Margaret Thatcher, endorsing the wisdom of the Conservative Party in choosing her as leader and strengthening her hold upon the party. The election again disappointed the Liberals and gave another severe blow to the Scottish Nationalists, whose hopes were already waning after their reverse in the devolution referendum in the previous year. Parties must do their utmost at elections then because there is much to win or lose and because their efforts can influence the result. However, they must commit themselves totally not just from self-interest but out of political conviction, for elections are at the heart of the liberal-democratic process. They constitute the supreme symbol of a society's commitment to the democratic method by which power changes hands peacefully – 'by ballots not bullets' – and governments are made accountable to the people.

The governing party generally tries to manipulate the economy to its own benefit and then use its control over the date of the election to maximum advantage. The assumption is that people whose standard of living is improving will reward it with another spell in office. This simple strategy appears to have worked in 1955, 1959, 1966, and in October 1974. In 1979, the position was different. Dependent on only a slender majority, the Labour Government was pushed by defeat in the House of Commons into holding a general election earlier than it wished. It thereby lost the advantage normally conferred by the governing party's control over the timing of elections. With hindsight, the prime ministerial decision not to call an election in October 1978 probably destroyed Labour's chances of achieving even a narrow victory in its final year of office.

In early 1983, circumstances were again unusual, but for different reasons.[1] Like Labour in 1978, the Conservatives were in their fourth year of office and faced a decision about whether to go to the electorate then, or wait until later in that year or even the following year. But whereas, according to a MORI poll (Market and Opinion Research International), Labour in 1978 trailed by 2 per cent in the polls, the Conservatives in 1983 held a 12 percentage point lead. However, the party enjoyed this considerable advantage not because of its success in running the economy – indeed, Gross Domestic Product (GDP) was less than two points higher in the second quarter of 1983 than it had been three years earlier whilst unemployment had more than doubled to 12·5 per cent. The advantage lay rather in the 'Falklands factor', for the military victory gained over Argentina in June 1982 had a dramatic effect on the Conservative Government's fortunes. Before the event, it lay 1·5 percentage points behind Labour and 3·5 percentage points behind the Alliance; by the autumn of 1982, however, its popularity had rocketed, and it held a 13 point lead over Labour and an even larger 19·5 point advantage over the Alliance. The second unusual circumstance profiting the Conservatives was the hopeless weakness of the opposition party arising out of the divisive formation of the Alliance. On the other hand, the emergence of a new party had also introduced an element of uncertainty into the political system, and there was widespread talk amongst political commentators of the possibility of the next election producing a situation in which no party had an overall majority – a 'hung' parliament. The decision, therefore, about when to call the election was rather less clear-cut than it appeared. Abroad, Socialist parties had done well during the economic recession, winning elections in France, Spain, Sweden and Australia. However difficult it might be to squander its huge lead, the problem still remained for the Conservative Party of minimising its chances of doing so. The question of timing still arose. To go to the country too late risked forfeiting the beneficial effects of the 'Falklands factor': not surprisingly, Conservative Party organisation favoured an early election. But to go too soon risked opposition taunts that the Conservatives were using patriotism for party purposes and also that they were 'cutting and running', that is, refusing to serve out their full term of office, knowing that the economic indicators were going to get worse.

By 7 May, when Conservative leaders and officials met at Chequers, the position was clearer. The massive rise in Alliance popularity during the Bermondsey by-election had subsided and the threat – from the Conservative viewpoint – that Labour might replace its leader, Michael Foot, by the more dangerous Denis Healey had receded after Labour's victory in the Darlington by-election. The redrawing of constituency boundaries by the Boundary Commission seemed likely to benefit the Conservatives by as much as thirty seats. The recent local government by-election confirmed the mediocre prospects of the Alliance. Government figures showed inflation down to 4 per cent. It was an opportune moment. On 9 May, Mrs Thatcher announced that the election would take place one month later. Both opinion polls and bookmakers confirmed the wisdom of her judgement. MORI gave the Conservatives a 15 point lead over Labour and a 25 point lead over the Alliance on 11 May. Ladbrokes made the Conservatives 5–1 on to win with Labour at 3–1 against and the Alliance at 50–1 against. Barring quite exceptional misfortune, the Conservatives would win. The main interest focused, there-fore, on the margin of their victory and the performance of the Alliance.

Labour then had even fewer grounds for optimism than in 1979. In order to achieve the narrowest winning margin con-ceivable – an overall majority of one – it required a 'swing' of 5·4 per cent, a bigger 'swing' than any party had achieved in the post-war period. Unlike 1979, when the party had a more popular leader than the Conservatives, this time its leader was well behind in popularity: it did not even have the option therefore of fighting a 'presidential-style' campaign. Moreover, in the inter-vening years the party had been damaged by the defection of the SDP and by an ineffectual struggle to get rid of the Militant tendency, a Trotskyite group which formed a party within a party. As often happens when it is in opposition, the party had swung strongly to the left – a shift which was given additional impetus in this case by the radicalisation of public sector workers under the impact of Conservative economic policies and by the resurgence of the Campaign for Nuclear Disarmament. Clearly, its public reputation for division and 'extremism' would be hard to overcome. In addition, its private polls were gloomy, suggesting not only that the party lacked credibility but also that public opinion neither blamed the Conservatives for unemployment nor believed that increased public spending was an answer to the country's problems. As for the Alliance, its high pre-Falklands hopes had virtually evaporated. On any realistic analysis, it was likely to lose some of its forty-two seats, the twenty-nine SDP seats (most of which had been won in Labour not SDP colours) being particularly vulnerable. Really, the most it could hope for was to hold the balance of power in a deadlocked parliament. In that event, it decided it would support a minority government of any complexion which would stay in the EEC, adopt an expansionist economic programme and hold a referendum on proportional representation in two years.

Behind the unruffled public face the parties strove to present, there were strains, expecially in the opposition parties. When the Labour Party is out of power, the transformation of its programme into a manifesto is the joint responsibility of the Shadow Cabinet and the National Executive Committee (NEC). In 1979, James Callaghan, the leader, vetoed several left-wing proposals at the last minute. Later this led to charges that the Labour leaders did not 'believe' in the party programme, a row that Michael Foot was determined to avoid on this occasion. Denis Healey insisted on the insertion of promises to cooperate with NATO on defence spending and to include Polaris in future arms negotiations. But this was the only success achieved by right-wingers in modifying what they saw as an extreme left-wing document. At an NEC–Shadow Cabinet meeting on 11 May, Foot curtailed discussion to one hour on the grounds that there was no time to redraft or polish the draft manifesto. The Shadow Chancellor, Peter Shore, is reported to have expressed his disappointment by calling the 15,000 word manifesto, entitled *The New Hope for Britain*, the 'longest suicide note in history'. On the face of it, the job facing the Alliance was even more difficult: getting two parties to agree on a manifesto. But the task was eased by the parties' public commitment to cooperation – the joint manifesto was called *Working Together for Britain*. It was also assisted by the determination of both leaderships to keep the manifesto in the hands of MPs and by the willingness of the Liberal leader, David Steel, to accept the SDP leader, Roy Jenkins, as effectual leader of the Alliance with the title of 'Prime Minister Designate'. But the process was still a complex one. An initial draft by an SDP member, Chris Smallwood, went in quick succession before separate SDP and Liberal groups, a joint SDP-Liberal coordinating committee, and the respective Chief Whips before final decision by the party leaderships and Chief Whips. The speed and parliamentary domination of the writing of the manifesto in the hands of MPs and by the willingness of the felt their views had not received the consideration merited by their campaigning skills. Both the more hierarchical structure and ethos of the party and its position in government ensured a smoother passage for the Conservative manifesto, *The Challenge of our Times*. As early as February, Cabinet ministers were asked for suggestions for inclusion in the manifesto and by the time it was discussed by a small group consisting of Mrs Thatcher, Sir Geoffrey Howe, Cecil Parkinson, the Party Chairman, and Ian Gow, the PM's Parliamentary Private Secretary, towards the end of the second week in April, the manifesto had gone through several drafts. Although Cabinet ministers saw the sections concerning their particular departments, only a small number – Sir Geoffrey Howe, Nigel Lawson, Norman Tebbit, Sir Keith Joseph and David Howell – saw the final draft. But if there were doubts in any section of the party about the final document, none of it reached the press.

The manifestoes put forward strongly contrasting policies. On the economy, both opposition groups called for expansion: Labour proposed an £11 billion programme aimed at reducing unemployment to under 1 million within five years; the Alliance advocated economic reflation designed to cut the jobless figures by 1 million over the same period. The Conservative manifesto gave priority to the fight against inflation rather than the reduction of unemployment. The Party claimed credit for bringing inflation down and promised to reduce it further by maintaining firm control of public spending and the money supply. On the EEC, however, the Alliance was closer to the Conservatives than to Labour. Whereas Labour proposed withdrawal from the European Community within the lifetime of a single parliament, the Alliance and the Conservatives were committed to continuing membership. On defence, Labour was for a non-nuclear policy but both the Conservatives and the Alliance supported the retention of Britain's nuclear deterrent. However, there were differences within this broad framework. Whereas both made the deployment of Cruise missiles in Britain depend on the negotiating position adopted by the USSR in coming arms talks, the Alliance went much further than the Conservatives towards scaling-down the role of nuclear weapons in British and European defence, proposing the cancellation of Trident and the establishment of a battlefield nuclear-weapon-free zone extending over 95 miles in Europe.

Each party devised a campaign strategy appropriate to its political situation. Knowing that they needed only to avoid serious mistakes in order to win, the Conservatives deliberately fought a low-key campaign. They stressed the determined leadership of Mrs Thatcher, and sought to nullify the argument that it was time for a change by pointing out that she had successfully begun her task and now required a second term of office to complete it. They attacked the Labour manifesto as the most extreme ever put before the British electorate and drew attention to its inconsistency on defence policy. Labour hit back on jobs and the welfare state. The Conservatives, they argued, could not shuffle off responsibility for high unemployment on to the world recession: Tory policies were also in part to blame. Labour itself gave the highest priority to the fight against unemployment. Drawing attention to the Conservatives' well-publicised preference for private housing, health and education, they predicted further cuts in collective provision and suggested the welfare state was not safe in Tory hands. The Alliance attacked the Conservative record on unemployment and the welfare state and Labour for its 'one-sided' disarmament proposals and its threatened withdrawal from the EEC, the consequence of which would be an isolationist and virtually neutralist Britain. These three parties fought nationwide campaigns throughout Britain (although not in Ulster). Welsh and Scottish voters had the further possibility of voting Nationalist: Plaid Cymru criticised Labour for 'centralism' and the Conservatives for unfair exploitation of Welsh resources (water supplies); the Scottish National

Party (SNP) called once again for Scottish oil to be put to more effective use (i.e. in Scotland). In some (mainly English) constituencies, voters might have an even wider choice. Extreme right parties ran 113 candidates (National Front sixty, British National Party fifty-three) and at the other end of the political spectrum, the Communist Party put forward thirty-five and the Workers Revolutionary Party, twenty. The largest minor party was the Ecology Party with 108 candidates. There was the usual range of 'fringe' parties and candidates representing a rich variety of causes, including Cornish nationalism, Wessex regionalism (self-government for Wessex), noise abatement, the restoration of capital punishment, prosperity for all, traditional English food and justice for divorced fathers. There was a fancy dress party and three kinds of loony party.

All three main parties directed their campaigns at the media and at the 'marginal' constituencies. They aimed to grab the headlines in the main evening news bulletins and in the newspapers next day and to that end they held early morning press conferences and engaged in publicity stunts such as Mrs Thatcher's visits to a Cornish farm, a Berkshire electronics factory and a Newcastle bakery. All appointed campaign committees whose tasks included analysis of the opinion polls, the briefing of leaders for the press conferences and general oversight of the progress and tactics of the campaign. All used advertising firms to help present their 'messages': the Conservatives called upon the services of Saatchi and Saatchi; Labour used Wright and Partners; and the Alliance the Gold, Greenlees and Trott agency. As well as keeping a close watch on the national opinion polls, the parties used private polls to identify key issues and to 'monitor' their campaigns. When in the later stages of the election, the Alliance tried to engineer a final swing of opinion in its favour by 'talking up' a slight movement towards it in the polls, Labour countered by releasing its own private polls which did not suggest such a trend and by criticising the 'telephone' polls which were encouraging the Alliance. After attending their morning press conferences, the respective leaders campaigned the country, travelling to their venues in sharply-contrasting styles; Mrs Thatcher by plane or well-appointed charabanc; Michael Foot by car; and David Steel in the Liberal 'battle-bus'. Whereas the Labour, Liberal and SDP leaders engaged in 'walkabouts', Mrs Thatcher avoided them. Although she did address impromptu open-air meetings on several occasions, fears for her safety as well as a desire to avoid interruptions by 'rent-a-crowd' hecklers led to her six major speeches of the campaign being made to all-ticket audiences.

The media responded by giving the campaign extensive coverage. An eve of campaign meeting settled the allocation of time for 'party politicals' in the ratio of five Conservative, five Labour, four Alliance. The Alliance had requested parity of treatment in view of its by-election record and intention to contest all mainland seats. Minor parties fielding over fifty candidates (Ecology, National Front, British National Party) qualified for one radio and one TV broadcast each; the SNP got two broadcasts and Plaid Cymru one in their respective countries. It is hard to judge the effects of these transmissions but one commentator – the visiting American broadcaster, Walter Cronkite – described them as ranging 'from terrible to barely tolerable'. Coverage of the election made up over 50 per cent of the output of the daily news bulletins. The party leaders appeared at regular intervals – to be questioned by the media professionals on Panorama, Weekend World and TV Eye and by ordinary voters on Nationwide and Election Call. An ordinary voter caused the most embarrassment to a politician during the campaign when quizzing Mrs Thatcher on the sinking of the Argentine cruiser, *General Belgrano*, on Nationwide. The press was overwhelmingly Conservative and hostile to Labour and the Alliance. Only two of the seventeen national newspapers supported Labour and about three-quarters of the electorate read newspapers which supported a Conservative victory. The 'tabloid' press was hostile to the Alliance and the 'quality' newspapers, although more sympathetic, were unprepared to back it unreservedly. The Alliance also received in general a less advantageous proportion of news coverage in the press than on the air, the ratio being five Conservative, five Labour, two Alliance. Perhaps this mattered less because the great majority of people regarded election reporting in the press as both more biased and less interesting than on TV.

Efforts to direct resources to 'marginal', 'critical' or 'winnable' seats were made difficult by the redrawing of constituency boundaries and, in the cases of Labour and the Alliance, by shortage of funds. There were significant differences in overall expenditure, the Conservatives spending £5·7 million (£3·6 million nationally, of which £2·8 million went on advertising, £2·1 million locally), Labour £4.1 million (£2.2 million centrally and £1.9 million in the constituencies) and the Alliance £1·4 million (£850,000 centrally, £550,000 locally). However, an even greater imbalance existed in the spread of professional party organisers. Labour had full-time agents in forty-three constituencies and a further eighteen constituencies shared nine agents between them. But few of its agents were in the 105 seats it had identified as key marginals. The Liberals had only twenty-two full-time agents; elsewhere, the Alliance, like Labour, had to rely on local volunteers. Against this, the Conservatives had 332 agents covering 357 constituencies, which included all but eight of its 100 'critical' seats.

Pressure groups were active both inside and outside the parties. The Trade Unions for Labour Victory, a group of unions under the leadership of David Basnett, the General Secretary of the General and Municipal Workers Union, gave considerable financial support and, in some parts of the country, administrative help to Labour's election effort. The Campaign for Nuclear Disarmament (CND), the Welsh Language Society, the public sector unions, consumer, abortion, Third World, animal welfare and anti-cruel sports groups all pressed their cases. CND was the most active of these groups. It hoped to force the issue of British acceptance of Cruise and Trident missiles to the forefront of the campaign by national press advertisements, window posters, door to door leafleting and speaking tours by its leaders. Whilst CND refused to make the transition from pressure group to political party by rejecting the defence minister's challenge to field its own candidates, some of its supporters did decide to help the Labour campaign.

During the election, events occurred to cause the parties varying degrees of embarrassment. Denis Healey's statement that Polaris should be included in the Geneva Disarmament negotiations apparently contradicted Labour's manifesto commitment to unilateral nuclear disarmament. This raised a question which was never satisfactorily resolved: if nuclear weapons were going to be abandoned anyway, how could they be used as bargaining counters in arms negotiations? Or, put another way, if the proposal to scrap them drew no parallel concessions from the USSR, was it not logical to retain them? The Conservatives were embarrassed by the 'leak' of three documents on public expenditure policy, the most damaging of which suggested that the government was considering ending direct state financing of education and the replacement of the National Health Service by private health insurance. These revelations led Labour to attact what it described as the Conservatives' 'hidden' or 'real' manifesto, i.e. the one the party dare not publish which threatened the whole structure of the welfare state. There were other awkward moments; a draft report of the House of Commons Treasury and Civil Service Committee, chaired by a Conservative, Edward du Cann, attributed a large part of the rise in unemployment during Mrs Thatcher's term of office to the over-valuation of sterling (which the government could influence) as compared with the government's own claim that the job losses were the result of the world recession (which it could not affect). The publication of an advertisement directed at coloured people with the caption 'Labour says he's black. Tories say he's British' caused offence to ethnic minorities who considered themselves to be both black and British. The story that an ex-National Front member was the Conservative candidate for Stockton South lessened the force of Conservative attacks on Labour Party extremism in running Militant candidates. The main worry for the Alliance was less an event than a 'non-event' – the obstinate refusal of the opinion polls to move decisively in its direction. Accordingly, the Liberal and SDP leaders met at Ettrick Bridge (the home of David Steel) late in the campaign with the intention of making morale-boosting changes. But Roy Jenkins, who, as Prime Minister Designate, had made little impact on the campaign, refused to stand down from that position in favour of David Steel and the only consequence of the meeting was that David Steel took a more prominent role, and Roy Jenkins a more subdued one, for the rest of the campaign.

The Conservatives won the election on a 3·8 per cent swing, gaining an overall majority of 144 seats in the House of Commons, their largest since the war (see Table 1.1). The result was a personal triumph for Mrs Thatcher and a disaster for Michael

12   Parties and Pressure Groups

Table 1.1 *The 1983 general election*

	Total votes	Share of total	MPs
Conservative	13,012,602	42·4	397
Labour	8,460,860	27·6	209
Alliance	7,776,065	25·4	23
SNP	331,975	1·1	2
Plaid Cymru	125,309	0·4	2
Others	962,692	3·1	17
Total	30,669,503	100·0	650
Electorate	42,197,344		
Turnout	72·7%		

Source: *The Times*, 11 June 1983

Foot and Roy Jenkins, who soon resigned the leaderships of their respective parties. Francis Pym, the Foreign Secretary, and several other ministers, also lost their jobs in a post-election reshuffle. Parties began their post-mortems. Compared with 1979, Labour had lost nearly 3 million votes and fifty-nine seats. Would it have fared better under a different leader? The Alliance had polled extremely well – only three-quarters of a million votes fewer than Labour – but had ended up with 186 fewer seats. Discussion inevitably followed on the fairness of the British electoral system and the advantages and disadvantages of a possible remedy such as proportional representation. Other, equally serious, matters were raised in the post-election inquest. The British system of government works best with a powerful opposition. But was not any opposition which was so numerically inferior likely to be an ineffective one? And, if so, was this not likely to make government more autocratic? And, further, in the event of a weak opposition, was not the strongest resistance of government policies likely to come from its own backbenchers or even from outside parliament – from pressure groups, for example? Further, how could anti-Conservative forces, divided as they were, ever mount a serious challenge again?

It is clear that this case study has raised important questions about the character of parties and pressure groups and their respective roles in the political system. It will be a central concern of this book to provide answers to such questions. But, first, what are parties and pressure groups and what tasks do they perform in political life?

Political parties

When Harold Wilson resigned as Prime Minister in March 1976, according to constitutional convention it was the Queen's constitutional prerogative to send for his successor. In fact, she had to 'choose' on advice the leader of the party with a majority in the House of Commons. This meant that she had to wait for the Labour Party to select its new leader before she could act. The constitutional facade hid the reality of party. The summons to the Palace was a formality, the role of the Queen purely symbolic. The formal political institutions – parliament and the monarchy – mattered less than the informal institution, the political party.

A major task of political parties is to seek political power: to exercise it if they win it or to influence or criticise the government if they fail to. Parties recruit politicians. They play a key role in the selection of parliamentary candidates, largely determining who will stand for election. They also select leaders. The fact that political leaders are chosen by parties obviously influences the sort of leader who emerges. For parties wish to survive: they therefore try to pick election winners or, at least, someone who will hold the party together. They have distinctive traditions and ideas and attempt to pick leaders who will express these self-images. Parties also formulate policies and draw up programmes. They exist to get things done and to prevent changes they dislike. As Burke wrote: 'Party is a body of men united for promoting by their joint endeavour the national interest upon some principle in which they are all agreed.' In drawing up their proposals, they go beyond the ideas of their own supporters to consider the suggestions of other groups and individuals in society. They collect and select from a great variety of policy proposals.

Parties form governments. The hope of governing in the not too distant future sustains parties just as the hope of government office buoys up their individual members. Of course, not all parties have an equal chance of forming a government, but government is always by *some* party. It is true that when a party leader becomes Prime Minister his power rests on a broader base than party and he must behave as a national leader and not solely in the interests of his party. Nor does the governing party always carry out the whole of its programme. But the system may still be described as party government. In Britain the parties effect the constitutional requirement that the government should command a majority in the House of Commons.

Constitutional opposition is also a matter of party. The party with the second highest number of parliamentary seats in the UK forms both the official opposition to the government and the alternative government. This political practice developed during the nineteenth century. Before then, opposition to the King's Government, unless it was equated with faction and condemned altogether, was carried out by parliament as a whole. By 1867, however, opposition had become both formalised and attached to party. In the words of one late-Victorian writer, the opposition party constituted the main check on 'a presumptuous government and a hasty legislature'.[2]

This is to view parties primarily from a Westminster perspective. Parties are, of course, much more than agencies of government and opposition. They are also popular institutions which reach right down to the localities, to the grass-roots of politics. They are the prime vehicles of political representation. In the 1983 general election over 30 million people voted. On one theory of the constitution, they voted for the best person to represent their constituencies in parliament. But this theory is out-of-date. What has made it out-of-date is not only the extensions of the franchise following 1867 but also the rise of parties. The two changes go together, for parties enable the enlarged electorate to make meaningful choices. Parties make mass franchise democracy possible; they do so by narrowing down the alternatives at elections. The voter may never have heard of a particular candidate before, but he has heard of the Conservative, Labour and Liberal parties, the Scottish and Welsh Nationalist parties, the Communist Party and the National Front. Parties group candidates together in a coherent way so that votes in one constituency can be related to votes in another. Elections, therefore, are truly 'general', not just a series of separate actions. Parties enable the wishes of voters, crudely reduced and simplified, to be translated into action.

Parties provide a means of communication between government and citizens more permanent than an opinion poll. People need organisations if they are to make their voices heard in politics. They cannot choose when to be consulted in a referendum and, so far as individual voters are concerned, opinion polls are taken randomly. A person may well have sensible ideas on public policy but without an organisation to back them these ideas are likely to wither away. A minimal precondition of political influence, therefore, is a party or pressure group. Parties also enable politicians to sound out the opinions of ordinary citizens, although they are less important for this purpose than opinion polls or the 'surgeries' of MPs. They are two-way channels of communication between rulers and ruled. Parties adopt the suggestions of individuals and groups and shape them to their own purposes; they also use their machinery to impart their own ideas to their supporters and to the electorate at large; indeed, an important aspect of party activity is to provide a forum of debate and an education in political reality. Parties both represent and mobilise political opinion.

Finally, parties are agencies of political participation. So widespread are they that it is tempting to think of a tendency to form parties as an inevitable phenomenon, but in fact it cannot be said that there is anything inevitable about their emergence since they are absent from about one-quarter of the countries of the world. Of course, the meaning of party membership varies a great deal. In the USSR, to be a Communist Party member is to belong to the privileged ruling elite. Communist parties not in power try to gain an almost total commitment from their members. By contrast, party membership means much less in a moderate political party: usually merely the payment of a small subscription and the holding of a membership card. In the United States, the notion of party membership is even vaguer; supporters may become 'members' of a particular party merely by declaring, when they register as voters for primary elections, that they have voted for that party in the past or intend to do so in the future. In fact, identification with a political party need not entail actual membership. To vote for a party in a local or national election may reflect a lesser commitment than that of a dues-paying or card-carrying member, but is nonetheless a way for the individual to assert a distinct political identity. Parties are the primary agencies of political participation for citizens of modern states, and are likely to remain so.

It is hard to see how a liberal-democratic political system could work without a system of political parties. They form the main if not the only means of political recruitment, representation, communication and participation. They form governments and oppositions. The public agrees about their importance. In a survey conducted in 1975–76 for the Houghton Committee on Financial Aid to Political Parties, 55 per cent 'agreed strongly' with the proposition that parties are essential to our form of national government and 31 per cent 'agreed a little' with this statement; only 8 per cent disagreed in any way at all.

Pressure groups

The term 'pressure group' is normally used to denote the other type of informal political organisation whose activities have a great influence on national decision-making processes. Pressure groups try to achieve by political action changes which they see as desirable, and to prevent changes regarded as undesirable. Two excellent examples are business groups and the trade unions. These are the leading interest (or 'sectional') groups in which membership is based on the performance of a specific economic role: for example, work as a miner or a company director. Sectional groups 'protect' the interests of their members. Another common type of group is the *promotional* group (sometimes also called the 'cause' or 'attitude' group). Such groups are held together by a shared attitude; they seek to promote a particular cause; Shelter and the Child Poverty Action Group are good examples of promotional groups. In our case study, the Campaign for Nuclear Disarmament could also be described in this way. Sometimes, the term 'pressure group' is used less precisely. For example, government departments (or, indeed, any other organisation which seeks political influence) are sometimes loosely said to be acting as pressure groups. Thus, the term can refer to a form of activity as well as denoting a type of organisation (the sense in which it is generally used throughout the rest of this book).

Pressure groups are unlike parties in that they rarely stand for office and have no aspirations to form a government. They do not put forward candidates at elections and they do not seek to exercise power directly. As we saw in the case study, CND refused the challenge to provide candidates for election. Some people mistakenly say that the leader of a powerful trade union has as much political influence as the Prime Minister but in fact neither he nor any other pressure group leader seeks to be Prime Minister or to occupy any other government office. This difference has important implications for the behaviour of parties and pressure groups. There are, of course, parties which are based upon a single narrow interest – farmers' parties in some European countries are an obvious example – and which are consequently in this respect rather like pressure groups. Usually, however, parties propose policies over a wide range of issues. More significantly still, they seek power through the electoral system; they govern; and they fill other formal constitutional roles such as that of HM Opposition. Finally, although pressure groups do seek political influence, this is not necessarily the primary concern of their memberships. Thus churches exist for the cure of souls, universities for the cultivation of minds, the trade unions to raise wages and improve working conditions, the motoring organisations to provide breakdown and other services. In relation to politics, all these institutions are 'marginal' and, even though the degree of their political orientation varies, most groups are politically marginal (or 'partial') in this sense.

These differences in aims and character between parties and pressure groups are often overlooked because in many respects their functions in the political process are similar. Both parties and pressure groups are agencies of political representation, communication and participation; moreover, pressure groups often have close organisational links with parties. The Labour Party, for example, has been described as 'two-thirds pressure group, one-third political party' because of its relationship with the trade unions; similarly there are strong informal links between business interests and the Conservative Party. But similarity of functions and frequent formal and informal links or over-lapping should not be allowed to obscure the fact that parties seek to exercise political power directly whereas pressure groups do not.

The impact of the big pressure groups on government in recent years will be discussed later. It is sufficient here to notice that the practice of functional representation – that is, representation by trade or profession – has become widely accepted since the war. It is recognised that governments both should and do consult with affected interests before making decisions; conversely, those interests could be said to have a right to be so consulted. A pressure group has to include the bulk of the people, organisations and companies in the sphere of its concern in order to be acceptable to government as spokesman for that interest; in return for its acceptance as official spokesman a group has to agree to keep negotiations confidential even from its own members. Not all groups achieve this legitimacy but the system as a whole has gained widespread acceptance. Nonetheless, the emergence of functional representation raises important political and constitutional questions. For many people dislike the practice of making crucial social and economic decisions in this way – that is, through private consultations between government and groups before parliament is informed – and would like to get parliament 'back in the act'.

How has the system of functional representation come about? The most significant factor has been the needs of post-war governments faced for the first time with the management of the economy and of a welfare state. They have had to consult with the occupational groups vital to the success of their enterprise. Another reason has been the attitudes of the Conservative and Labour parties: both are sympathetic to the idea that important interests should have direct representation in the counsels of government. Each party has a collectivist theory of representation and each has traditionally seen itself as the vehicle by which specific social groups (the propertied and working classes respectively) can exercise political influence. They have consequently had no difficulty in accepting the idea that these groups (and others) may legitimately wield that influence *outside* parliament.

Thus, this book is about the contemporary British parliamentary democracy as party government and group representation. Its main concerns will be the character of the political parties and the leading pressure groups and their relationships with each other. It also examines their impact on the system as a whole and their contribution to governmental effectiveness and citizen participation.

2 Parties and the Political System

The party system

It is useful to distinguish between parties which have a chance of governing the country and those which do not. In terms of *government*, the United Kingdom has had a two-party system for most of the period since 1945. The two major parties have alternated in power: Labour, 1945–51; Conservative, 1951–64; Labour, 1964–70; Conservative, 1970–74; 1974–79, Labour; from 1979, Conservative again. Until the early 1970s, many people spoke of the British two-party system as almost 'natural': it was taken for granted. In 1977, however, Labour lost its overall parliamentary majority and, to prevent repeated defeats in the House of Commons, formed a pact with the Liberal Party. The Liberals did not actually enter the government as they would have done if a coalition had been formed. Nonetheless, the pact of February 1977 signalled a crack in the two-party system of government. In fact the crack did not widen. The sizeable majority won by the Conservatives in the 1979 general election and the even larger majority gained in 1983 relegated the incident to minor significance. And the Liberal-SDP Alliance may need a change in the electoral system itself if it is ever to form a government.

In terms of *electoral choice,* there is a multi-party system. The two major parties are flanked by a number of minor parties – the Liberals, the SDP, the Scottish and Welsh Nationalists, the Northern Ireland parties, the Communist Party of Great Britain, the National Front and the British National Party.

Of course, support for minor parties is often regionalised and, in the last three instances, small. Before 1983, only the Liberal Party of the various smaller parties contested elections on a national scale: in October 1974, for example, there were 619

Liberal candidates, only four fewer than each of the two major parties. In 1983, as we have seen, the Alliance fought all 633 seats in mainland Britain. But the Scottish National Party (SNP), Plaid Cymru and the Ulster parties are limited to their respective areas. A vote for these parties certainly expresses a political preference, but it does not help to choose a government as none of them has a realistic chance of becoming the government of the UK. Sometimes, votes for the smaller parties are spoken of as 'protest' votes – a point which should not be pressed too far for the minor parties on the mainland and is even less valid for Northern Ireland.

Ultimately, of course, no hard and fast line separates the types of party. It is votes which decide whether a smaller party becomes a major party and the Alliance, the National Front and the Communist Party of Great Britain could all, in theory, become governing parties. Equally, there is no reason why citizens of Scotland and Wales should not express their opinions by voting for the SNP or Plaid Cymru.

The political history of the UK does not always fit in well with the picture of two major parties taking it in turns to govern. There have been several coalitions (1916–22; 1931–40; 1940–45). Moreover, for significant periods (1910–16; 1924; 1929–31) a government drawn from one party was dependent on the support of a third party. During the first half of the twentieth century Labour rose to the position of alternative governing party while the Liberal Party declined. For a time, however, the three parties all fought for political power and people spoke of 'the naturalness of the three-party system'. These parties were said to represent the three main political viewpoints of left, right and centre. In the same way, between 1945 and 1975, the two-party system was considered right because it expressed the two 'natural' political alternatives (left and right).

There were, then, many precedents for the more uncertain electoral and parliamentary politics of the 1970s. This decade saw a continuing decline in support for the two major parties and a rise in the followings of several minor ones. In 1951 the Conservative and Labour parties' combined share of the vote was nearly 97 per cent; in October 1974 it was down to 75 per cent (Labour, 39·2 per cent; Conservatives, 35·8 per cent). In other

Table 2.1 *The major parties: votes, parliamentary seats and share of the total vote, 1945–1983*

General election	Votes (to nearest ¼m)		Seats		Percentages of total vote (to nearest ¼%)	
	Lab.	Con.	Lab.	Con.	Lab.	Con.
1945	12	10	393	213	48	40
1950	13¼	12½	315	298	46	43½
1951	14	13¾	295	321	49	48
1955	12½	13¼	277	344	46½	49½
1959	12¼	13¾	258	365	44	49½
1964	12¼	12	317	304	44	43½
1966	13	11½	363	253	48	42
1970	12¼	13	287	330	43	46½
1974 Feb.	11½	11¾	301	297	37	38
1974 Oct.	11½	10½	319	277	39	36
1979	11½	13¾	268	339	37	44
1983	8½	13	209	397	27½	42½

Sources: D. Butler and A. Sloman, *British Political Facts, 1900–1975*, Macmillan pp. 184–6; *The Guardian*, 5 May 1979; *The Times*, 11 June 1983

words, Labour took office in October 1974 with the support of less than two-fifths of those who voted. Seven months previously, for the first time since 1929, no one party had achieved an overall majority and Labour had taken office as a minority government. Over the preceding twenty-five years, the two major parties had lost the support of about one-fifth of voters (see Table 2.1).

The smaller parties began to do well (Table 2.2). The Liberal share of the total vote rose from 7·5 per cent in 1970 to over 19 per cent in February 1974. However, because of the electoral system, the number of Liberal MPs rose only from six to four-teen. On proportional representation, the Liberals would have received 121 seats. Other parties, too, made significant advances; the SNP and Plaid Cymru had little electoral success before 1970; by October 1974 the SNP had eleven MPs, Plaid Cymru, three. Altogether, between 1966 and October 1974, minor party repre-sentation in the House of Commons increased from fourteen to thirty-nine. Moreover, in many other seats the SNP and the

Table 2.2 *The minor parties: votes, parliamentary seats and share of the total vote, 1945–1983*

General election	Votes (to nearest 1/4m)	Seats	Percentage of total vote
1945	3	34	11·8
1950	2¾	12	10·4
1951	1	9	5·8
1955	1	9	3·9
1959	1¾	7	6·8
1964	3½	9	12·5
1966	2¾	14	9·7
1970	3	13	10·7
1974 Feb.	7¾	37	25
1974 Oct.	7¼	39	25
1979	6	28	19·2
1983	9	44	29·9

Sources: as for Table 2.1

Liberals became the main challengers to either the Conservatives or Labour.

The general election of 1979 partially reversed this trend. The victory of the Conservative Party, with its forty-three seat overall majority and its lead of seventy-one seats over Labour, restored the pre-1974 situation of the clear parliamentary ascendancy of a single party. Together, the major parties increased their share of both seats – 607, compared with 596 in October 1974 – and votes – 81 per cent, compared with 75 per cent in the previous election. The minor parties lost ground, Plaid Cymru surrendering one seat, the Liberals, three and the Scottish National Party, by far the hardest hit, nine. Minor party parliamentary representation declined from the forty seats achieved during the lifetime of the 1974–79 government. But there was not a complete return to the pre-1974 situation: in seats (twenty-eight, compared with thirteen in 1970), votes (about 6 million compared with 3 million in 1970) and share of the vote (19·2 per cent, compared with 10·7 per cent in 1970), the minor parties were much stronger than they had been a decade previously. The Labour Party, with only 11·5 million votes and a 37 per cent share of the vote, failed to recover its 1960s position. And the two-party system as a whole remained less popular with the voters than it had been between 1945 and 1974.

In 1983, the two-party system suffered further erosion. Together, the Conservative and Labour parties gained a mere 70 per cent of the UK vote (Conservative 42·4 per cent, Labour 27·6 per cent). This low joint poll was largely the consequence of a large drop in the Labour vote. Whereas the Conservatives lost over half a million votes between 1979 and 1983, Labour support fell by 3 million. Although it won only twenty-three seats, the Alliance took 25·4 per cent of the total vote, a large increase on the 13·8 per cent share of the vote (and eleven seats) won by the Liberals in 1979. Moreover, the Alliance was second in two-thirds of the 397 Conservative seats, Labour was second in only one-third of them. To win back power, Labour would need to gain 116 seats which would require a 'swing' of 12 per cent, far larger

Table 2.3 *Effects of proportional representation on the distribution of parliamentary seats: 1983 general election*

	Actual seats	National PR
Conservative	397	277
Labour	209	180
Lib/SDP Alliance	23	166
SNP	2	7
PC	2	3

Source: John Curtice and Michael Steed in Appendix 2 of D. Butler and D. Kavanagh, *The British General Election of 1983,* Macmillan, p. 359

than any in the post-war period. In electoral, although not in parliamentary terms, a three-party system was now in existence. Table 2.3 gives an estimate of how proportional representation would have affected the result on the British mainland. It would have led to either minority or coalition government. Overall, including Northern Ireland, minor parties enjoyed their greatest success since 1945, gaining approximately 30 per cent of the total vote.

The major trends, then, in the electoral politics of the 1970s and 1980s have been first, a gradual, then rapid, decline in support for the Labour Party; second, the continuing ability of the Conservative Party to attract over two-fifths of the voters; and finally, the emergence on the scene of two third parties, the most spectacular example of this being the success of the Alliance in 1983, which led many commentators to speak of the appeance of 'a new three-party system'. Underlying these trends are more deep-lying changes. A declining proportion of voters is firmly committed to one or other of the two main parties. In 1964, 40 per cent of electors identified 'very strongly' with either the Conservative or the Labour Party; by 1979, only 19 per cent did. Moreover, the political allegiances of voters to any party are becoming more conditional. Whilst over four-fifths of voters (85 per cent) in 1979 thought of themselves as supporters of one of the three main parties, compared with over nine-tenths (92 per cent) in 1964, only one-fifth (21 per cent) identified 'very strongly' with any of the parties, compared with at least two-fifths (43 per cent) who had done so in 1964. This decrease in firm party partisanship has to be taken together with pronounced electoral volatility. As much as 50 per cent of voters appear to change their vote at least once in a decade; of voters participating in both the October 1974 and 1979 elections, one-fifth changed their vote.[1] Faced with such flux in the electorate, no party need lose hope.

Finally, although occupational class remains the principal social basis of British electoral politics, it is of declining significance. A process of class 'de-alignment' is taking place. A major trend has been the growth of Conservative support amongst skilled manual workers and trade unionists, that is, amongst groups traditionally regarded as Labour's 'natural' supporters. Table 2.4 shows support for the parties in 1983 within various categories of

Table 2.4 *Voting patterns in the 1983 general election*

	Class			Trade union		Sex		Age				
	ABC1	*C2*	*DE*	*Member*	*Non-member*	*Men*	*Women*	*18-24*	*25-34*	*35-54*	*55+*	*All*
All	40	31	29	25	75	48	52	13	20	32	34	100
Cons	55	40	33	31	48	42	46	42	40	44	47	44
Lab	16	32	41	39	24	30	26	33	29	27	27	28
Alln	28	26	24	29	25	25	27	23	29	27	24	26
Other	1	2	2	1	3	2	2	2	2	2	2	2

Source: MORI (13,926 in combined sample).

occupational class, members and non-members of unions, sex and age. It reveals the continuing strength of the link between occupational class and voting behaviour: the Conservatives polled especially well amongst the middle class – the managerial, professional and supervisory groups (ABC₁); Labour's greatest source of support was in the semi-skilled and unskilled working class (DE). But it also indicates the extent of class de-alignment. Two-fifths of skilled workers (C₂) voted Conservative, a higher percentage than voted Labour. A high proportion of trade unionists also voted Conservative. Taken together with the ability of the Alliance to win votes from all sections of the social spectrum, the table seems to suggest that class dealignment was damaging Labour more than its rivals.

The parties operate within a system. They are interdependent, continually influencing and being affected by the actions of one another. In parliament, for example, each party acts with one eye on what its rivals are doing. Harold Wilson's policy as Labour Prime Minister was 'to put the Tories on the defensive and always give them awkward choices.'[2] Similarly, the Conservative appeal to national unity in the general election of October 1974 was in part a ploy to draw off Liberal support. And Mrs Thatcher's somewhat surprising remark in the 1983 campaign to the effect that the Labour Party would never die was an attempt to stiffen Labour's backing and undermine a possible late surge for the Alliance which the Conservatives particularly feared. The next chapter examines in detail the character of the two major parties and the differences between them, and chapter 4 considers the minor parties which have burst with such dramatic results upon the political scene in the 1970s. The work of both parliament and government is profoundly affected by the character, size and number of parties, but before going on to examine the nature of the parties, we must take up the analysis begun in chapter 1 of the role of parties in the political system and ask in a little more detail what it means to speak of 'government and opposition by party'.

Party government and opposition

There is no clearer symbol of party government than the immediate installation, after a general election, of the victorious party leader at No. 10 Downing Street. In the weeks that follow, a new Cabinet is formed and many lesser government posts are allocated. In the case of an election where an existing government's mandate is renewed, the Prime Minister may take the opportunity to reshuffle the Cabinet, as in 1983. Government in the United Kingdom is by party, in two closely related senses: the occupation by party members of executive offices and the use of the machinery of government to implement party policies. The two are related in practice because the first is a precondition of the second. Logically, however, the two meanings are distinct, since party members could occupy such posts without using their powers to carry out party policy. In the United States, where party affiliation is more a device for allocating government jobs than for carrying out specific policies, one meaning is uppermost. But in Britain, government is by party in *both senses*.

A high proportion of the MPs in a party which wins a general election can expect some office in the new government. Indeed the amount of political patronage at the disposal of the Prime Minister has increased very considerably. Between 1900 and 1975 the number of posts to be allocated rose from 42 to 118. Some MPs cannot be considered, for various reasons ranging from administrative incompetence and political extremism to old age and ill-health. Nevertheless, about half the members of the victorious party normally receive a post of some kind. The vast majority of politicians who receive ministerial jobs will have served a long apprenticeship in the parliamentary party: the appointment of 'outsiders' such as Frank Cousins (to the Wilson

Government, 1964) and John Davies (by Heath, 1970) is rare. Party appointees form what has been described as the Prime Minister's 'pay-roll' vote in the House of Commons (that is, those upon whose loyalty he can rely with considerable certainty) and their existence in itself constitutes an important source of party cohesion.

Parties in government use their power to carry out many of the policies proposed in their manifestoes. They also take many other decisions according to distinguishable ideas and attitudes. There are, of course, obstacles to the fulfilment of manifesto promises: civil servants may object or even be deliberately obstructive.[3] In the 1970s both major parties brought 'political' advisers into government to try to prevent this. Pressure group opposition, economic difficulties, the demands of foreign governments and international financial institutions, and the shortcomings of ministers and of the policies themselves all may deflect governments from their aims. Nevertheless, ministers are expected to behave as party men. As Lord Boyle has written: 'Ministers are appointed with a party background. They belong with a party as well as to a government and they are appointed with the responsibility of making clear what their value-judgements are.'[4]

Richard Rose has shown that the Conservative and Labour parties in government (1970–74, 1974–79) carried out substantial proportions of their manifesto pledges. Rose argues that the Conservative Government carried out 80 per cent of its manifesto commitments, the Labour Government 54 per cent of its pledges.[5] However, as Rose also shows, the considerable degree to which parties do fulfil their manifesto commitments is compatible with some notable exceptions. The Wilson government cut local authority mortgage lending in 1975–6 after promising to increase it in its 1974 manifesto. The Heath government reversed its manifesto hostility to further nationalisation and statutory wage controls, a famous 'U-turn' which Mrs Thatcher was determined not to repeat in 1979–1983.[6]

Of course, many actions of British Governments do not relate to manifestoes. On some policy areas, the parties deliberately avoid commitments. Labour, for example, avoided any promise to introduce 'conscience' reforms in its 1964 manifesto. Issues are often unforeseeable, developing suddenly between elections. In

1959 the application to join the Common Market was not fore-
seen; nor, in 1974, was it expected that Labour would subsequently be able to retain office only with Liberal support. In fact,
it was the absence of a secure parliamentary majority between
1974 and 1979 that prevented Labour from carrying out its
manifesto pledges to nationalise ship-repairing and introduce a
wealth tax. However, party government requires only that a
reasonable proportion of these issues should be decided according to distinctive party ideas and attitudes. These party ideas will
be discussed shortly; first we must examine what it means to say
that political opposition is by party.

In formal terms, it is only the largest defeated party which
constitutes HM Opposition. In reality, the government may be
defeated by any combination drawn from the smaller parties and
governing party backbenchers as well as from the official opposition. Attention, therefore, must focus continually on the likelihood of dissentient MPs from all these sources forming into a
bloc which may inflict such a defeat.

The British system of loyal single-party parliamentary opposition has two main functions: to provide an alternative government and to organise criticism of the government of the day.
Since 1955 the opposition has organised in Shadow offices which
mirror those of government. Shadow spokesmen are required
both to keep a check on the activities of their particular ministers
and to develop their own party's policy in their areas of interest.
Often they will actually receive the department they have
'shadowed' when their party enters government, but this is no
more than a strong possibility.[7]

Much parliamentary business is conducted by mutual agreement between government and opposition. The opposition itself
has certain well-established perogatives. Thus, whereas the final
decision on the parliamentary timetable rests with the government, the opposition itself initiates debate on twenty-nine Supply
days in each session and can choose the subjects to be debated in
the reply to the Address from the Throne. The opposition may
also choose the subjects for debate on recess adjournment days
and in short evening adjournments. Representation on Commons
Committees is proportionate to party strength in the House.

There are strict limits to what the opposition may hope to

achieve. It is almost impossible to bring the government down, and, in practice, rather difficult to engineer a defeat in the House of Commons. The maximum time for which government legislation may be delayed is thirteen months. Normally, the government's majority automatically precludes its defeat, although the opposition may also have several reasons for not wishing to press its opposition too far. These include a realistic appreciation of the difficulties of governing, a desire not to 'spoil the game' by provoking excessive opposition as a counter-reaction when the roles are reversed, and a wish to avoid the adverse consequences of opposing popular legislation. If it does wish to make things difficult for a government, the opposition can try to disrupt its programme by a variety of methods. These include complaining about government use of its time, delaying tactics (such as frequent censure motions, stalling ploys at the committee stage and calls for frequent divisons at the second and third reading stages of Bills), and simply trying to make the government look foolish in debates and at Question Time. A vote of censure enables an opposition to force a debate on any subject at any time. By convention, votes of censure are used only once or twice a session.[8] This situation has led one MP to comment that 'Parliamentary Opposition is a kind of bloodless guerrilla warfare in which the enemy is obstructed in committee, harassed at Question Time, and never beaten in set-piece battles'. (Ray Fletcher, former MP for Ilkeston, Derbyshire).[9]

In normal circumstances, where the government possesses a working majority, defeats on the floor of the House are relatively rare. (See Table 2.5 for the majorities held by post-war governments). A government with a reasonable majority holds a number of weapons which enable it to get its way. It can use its superior voting strength to restrict the opposition's delaying power and it can cut short debate by closure, the selection of amendments and the allocation of time motions (the guillotine). Normally, government defeats depend on an unusual combination of circumstances, the principal precondition being the abstention or opposition of its own backbenchers. Between 1945 and 1970, no government was defeated in the House of Commons because of the dissenting votes of its own backbenchers. But the position changed in the 1970s. Cross-voting increased

Table 2.5 *Overall majorities of governments in the House of Commons,
1945–1983*

Size of majority before election	Date	Governing party after election	Size of majority after election
181	1945	Labour	146
142	1950	Labour	5
3	1951	Conservative	17
19	1955	Conservative	58
50	1959	Conservative	100
90	1964	Labour	4
2	1966	Labour	96
62	1970	Conservative	30
16	Feb 1974	Labour	-33
-35	Oct 1974	Labour	3
-21	1979	Conservative	43
33	1983	Conservative	144

Sources: 'Political Britain', *The Economist*, 1980; *The Times*, 11 June 1983

considerably during the 1970–74 parliament, when 20 per cent of all divisions contained dissenting cross-votes and abstentions and the Conservative Government (majority thirty) was consequently defeated on six occasions.[10]

The Labour Governments elected in February and October 1974 suffered defeats even more frequently. The circumstances were rather uncommon. The first of these governments lacked an overall majority and the tiny majority of the second one had disappeared by February 1977. Twenty-three of their defeats happened as a consequence of revolts by their own backbenchers; nineteen defeats were the result of combination by the opposition parties.[11] These reverses did not lead to the resignation of the government until 28 March 1979. Having sustained itself in office by a pact with the Liberals in 1977, the Labour Government eventually fell after a defeat on a Conservative 'no confidence' motion. The voting was very close: Ayes, 311 (279 Conservative, 13 Liberal, 11 Scottish National Party, 8 Ulster Unionist); Noes, 310 (303 Labour, 2 Scottish Labour, 3 Plaid Cymru, 2 Ulster Unionist).

The Conservative Governments elected in 1979 and 1983 possessed respectively respectable and very large majorities. But they still showed themselves to be vulnerable on occasions to the new assertiveness of backbenchers. Sometimes, the threat of revolt is sufficient to persuade the government to change its mind. For voting against the government in the division lobbies is the sanction underlying many other less dramatic attempts by government backbenchers to influence policy decisions, for example, in discussion with Ministers and Whips, in party meetings, by speaking against the front bench in debates, and by putting down early day motions critical of the leadership. The Labour Government of 1966–70 withdrew two major pieces of legislation on industrial relations and House of Lords reform because of the *threat* of defeat by its own backbenchers. After 1979, backbench pressure short of anti-votes in the division lobbies forced modification of government policy on such issues as MPs' pay, the immigration rules and student grants.

Much government legislation receives the tacit support of the opposition – when it fails to request a division. According to Richard Rose, there were no significant divisions against the government on 78 per cent of government bills between 1970 and 1979.[12] One important reason for this is that a considerable proportion of government legislation is about administration rather than policy, that is, it is concerned with deciding how to implement already established policies rather than with the policy itself. Thus, under 10 per cent of administrative bills were the subject of divisions in the 1970–79 period, but about one-third of policy bills were.[13] In 1969–70, the Conservative Party asked for a division on five of the twenty-three policy bills of the Labour Government and in the parliamentary session following the 1970 election, Labour seriously opposed about half of the Conservatives' policy bills. Some policy issues such as foreign affairs simply are less contentious than others such as welfare and trade union legislation; generally, therefore, it is only the latter which oppositions consider to be worth contesting. Even when they do seek to change government legislation, their degree of success tends to be small. J. A. G. Griffith has shown that, in three sample sessions between 1967 and 1971, fewer than one in twenty amendments moved by opposition MPs in committee or report stages were actually incorporated in the Bills.[14] Of 3,673 opposition amendments in these sessions, only 4·4 per cent were approved by the Commons. Similarly, a study of the 1968–69 session by Valentine Herman revealed that 'not a single major or important opposition amendment was accepted by the government'.[15] Of course, the government might itself adopt amendments moved *in the first instance* by the opposition: when these are included, four major and seventeen important amendments succeeded in the 1968–69 session. Some opposition amendments, moreover, are intended merely to probe and to evoke assurances from the government and are withdrawn when the probes have succeeded and the assurances have been given. Even so the total impact of the opposition remains very limited.

The British system of government, then, is accurately described as government – and opposition – by *party*. What holds parties together goes beyond their hope of office and influence to shared collective goals. Their differing goals emanate from contrasting purposes and ideologies. We turn now to explore the parties' differing character, beginning with the parties which have dominated British politics since 1945, the Conservative and Labour parties.

3 The Conservative and Labour Parties

Political beliefs, attitudes and policies

The two leading political parties differ significantly from each other but also share some common ground; in addition they differ within themselves. Each of these points influences the practice of British politics. The differences between the parties mean that British Government has to respond to sharply contrasting beliefs, policies and prejudices: an incoming Conservative Minister may in practice wish to change very few of the policies of his Labour predecessor, but the Civil Service has to be prepared for the possibility that he will wish to change a great deal. The similarities make for a considerable amount of continuity and bipartisanship – for example, the Labour Opposition firmly supported the military response of the Conservative Government to the Argentine invasion of the Falklands in 1982.

There is a certain overlap in the middle ground of politics, which is a matter of shared culture and social background as much as of agreement on specific policies. The differences *within* the parties mean that each is to a large extent a *coalition*. This signifies more than that opinion in both major parties may be divided at any given moment over a range of important issues into right, centre and left, as it usually can be. It means that the parties consist of combinations of more-or-less stable 'tendencies' (sets of attitudes) and permanent 'factions' (groups of politicians). Party policy is almost invariably a compromise between the various tendencies and groupings; party leaders have to modify their actions according to the actual or expected demands of these groups.

The parties have contrasting doctrines. They have differing views of the shape society ought and ought not to take. But their policies in practice are also powerfully influenced by considerations of electoral expediency ('What will go down well with the voters') and by their own perceptions of the interests which they really represent ('What will suit businessmen or trade unionists'). An examination of the manifestoes issued by the parties in 1983 reveals these factors at work.

The parties put forward sharply contrasting policies on all the main areas of public concern: the economy, defence, the EEC and the welfare state. They both identified unemployment as the major problem of domestic policy but proposed totally different ways of tackling it. Conservative economic strategy focussed on further privatisation, strict control of public expenditure and incentives to private enterprise. Labour on the other hand offered an £11 billion (eleven million millions) package of measures to expand the economy to be financed by North Sea oil revenues, a saving on unemployment benefits, restrictions on overseas investment and by borrowing. The parties also had differing approaches to the control of inflation. In order to achieve their promise of a further reduction in inflation, the Conservatives intended to continue their financial strategy of strict control of the money supply and of public sector spending. But they made no precise reference to how they would control wages. They simply stated that the 5 per cent improvement in living standards achieved in the previous four years would continue so long as sensible government policies were matched by sensible attitudes towards pay increases; they did promise to resist unreasonable pay claims. To prevent prices soaring, Labour said it would reduce Value Added Tax (VAT) and introduce a new Price Commission. On pay, a Labour Government would make a national economic assessment with the trade unions on the likely growth of national output and how it could be shared: it would cover the allocation of resources and the distribution of income between profits, earnings from employment, rents, social benefits and other incomes. Agreement with the unions, it was hoped, would enable the party to reach its goal of reducing unemployment to below one million in five years without unleashing another inflationary spiral. Labour did not intend to return to government-imposed wage restraint.

The most explicit and ambitious section of the Conservative manifesto was on privatisation. The party aimed to transfer

Rolls-Royce, British Airways, substantial parts of British Steel, British Shipbuilders and British Leyland and 51 per cent of British Telecom to private ownership. They also intended to make 'as many as possible' of Britain's airports into private sector companies; to introduce substantial private capital into the National Bus Company; and to transfer the British Gas Corporation's offshore oil interests into independent ownership. Another Conservative goal was to increase competition in the gas and electricity industries and to attract private capital into them. By contrast, Labour pledged to renationalise Britoil and to take a public stake in electronics, pharmaceuticals, health equipment and building materials. The party also proposed to create a public bank operating through post offices and asserted its preparedness to take one or more of the clearing banks into public ownership if they failed to cooperate with reforms. To the Conservatives, a more efficient private sector was the key to national economic regeneration. They promised a continuing effort to simplify the tax system and gave 'high priority' to further improvements in tax allowances and lower rates of income tax. They wished to encourage wider share ownership by lower taxes on savings and capital, more private direct investment by individuals in company shares and more employee share schemes. By contrast with the small role given to the state in Conservative plans, Labour accorded government a central role in industrial revival. This could be seen not only in its plans to increase public spending but also in its preparedness to use tariffs and quotas against excessive import penetration.

The difference between the two parties on defence could hardly have been sharper. The Conservatives believed strongly in the maintenance of nuclear weapons as an effective deterrent. Labour proposed to get rid of them. It would cancel Trident, refuse to deploy Cruise missiles and complete the removal of nuclear bases from Britain 'within the lifetime of the Labour Government'. The Conservatives called Labour's unilateralist position 'reckless and naïve'. They pledged to support negotiations to reduce the deployment of nuclear weapons but they intended to start deploying Cruise missiles by the end of 1983 if the Soviet Union did not agree to the West's proposal to eliminate this class of weapons. Labour would continue to support

NATO but would also work towards a nuclear-free zone in Europe. The party promised to withdraw from the EEC within a five-year span, a policy which the Conservatives described as a potential catastrophe. Conservative EEC policy centred on the fight to reduce Britain's contribution to the Brussels budget.

Nor were the parties any closer on social policy. Thus, whilst the Conservatives rejected as 'totally unfounded' Labour's charge that they intended to dismantle the welfare state, their proposals had a markedly different emphasis from those of Labour. Whereas Labour promised to expand welfare spending, the Conservatives stressed getting value for money for the taxpayer and for those whom the public services seek to help. The Conservatives defended their record on social security and the National Health Service. They intended to build new hospitals and to improve existing facilities. At the same time, they welcomed the growth in private health insurance and pledged themselves to encourage it together with the close partnership between the state and the private sectors. Labour promised to expand spending on the NHS by 3 per cent per annum in real terms and on the personal social services by 4 per cent per annum. Its first priority would be to help families with children: child benefit would be increased by £2 per week, index-linked, and paid weekly if required. The Conservatives promised to protect pensions and other long-term benefits against rising prices: Labour pledged itself to increase the state pension in November 1983 to protect it against inflation and also promised other reforms, including progress towards a common pension at sixty for men and women. Conservative housing policy was shaped by its goal of a property-owning democracy. The party declared its intention to offer many thousand more families the chance to buy their homes in the next parliament, to extend the right-to-buy scheme to include leasehold property and to introduce shared ownership schemes. In contrast, Labour proposed to end enforced council house sales and to give public landlords the right to buy back houses sold under the Tories on first resale. The party promised to introduce a freeze on council house rents for a full year, to restore council house subsidies and to carry out an immediate 50 per cent increase in the total local authority housing investment programme. Conservative educational policy stressed the need to widen parental choice of and influence over their children's schooling as the most effective way of raising educational standards. Schools would be encouraged to keep proper records of their pupils' achievements and to carry out external graded tests; the public examinations system would be improved. Labour pledged the repeal of the 1979 Education Act. (This placed a duty upon local authorities to take account of parental preferences on schools, introduced an assisted places scheme to allow selected local authority pupils to attend independent schools and relaxed the statutory obligation on local education authorities [LEAs] to provide school milk, school meals and free school transport.) It also promised to prohibit all forms of academic selection in secondary schools.

Behind each manifesto is a characteristic and contrasting set of ideas, attitudes and self-images. Both parties in office have to administer a mixed economy, but Labour favours public enterprise, the Conservatives, private enterprise. Labour advocates greater social and economic equality; the Conservatives, feeling that social and economic inequality is inevitable, would like to enhance individual freedom. Labour bases its programme on cooperation and collective endeavour; the Conservatives emphasise self-help, individual responsibility and voluntary effort. Labour policy depended upon close collaboration with the trade union movement. Their manifesto promised to introduce industrial democracy.

The Conservatives had a different view of the unions. They proposed further trade union reform because, in their view, some trade union leaders still used their power against the wishes of their members and the interests of society. Accordingly, they proposed to give members of trade unions the right to hold ballots for the election of their leaders and to decide periodically whether their unions should have party political funds. They intended to curb the legal immunity of trade unions to call strikes without the prior approval of a secret ballot and proposed to hold further consultations about restricting the right to strike in essential services. Groups whose interests would be adversely affected by Labour's proposals included tax avoiders and tax evaders, the very wealthy (the richest 100,000), solicitors (who would lose their conveyancing monopoly), private schools (whose charitable status, tax privileges and public subsidies would be withdrawn) and members of the House of Lords (which would be forced to surrender its legislative powers). Labour was sympathetic to the unemployed, council tenants, families with children and disabled dependents, blind people, one-parent families and ethnic minorities. The party committed itself particularly to improve the position of women: it wanted to give women a genuine choice between looking after a family or going to work. It planned to introduce an Equal Pay Act, to strengthen the Sex Discrimination Act, to appoint a Cabinet Minister to promote equality between the sexes and to implement many other measures to help women. The Conservatives looked with special favour on small businessmen, investors and would-be share-holders, owner-occupiers, council tenants who wished to buy their houses, young people wanting farm tenancies, voluntary social workers, the police and the armed forces. Labour believed in the National Health Service and comprehensive education; the Conservatives reserved their greatest enthusiasm for private medical insurance and the independent schools. They promised firm action against purveyors of video nasties and young hooligans as well as against unrepresentative trade union leaders. They intended to abolish the Greater London Council (GLC) and six metropolitan authorities – described as a wasteful and unnecessary tier of government – as part of their policy of curing the mistakes of 'decades of town-hall socialism'.

A comparison of the manifestoes has revealed clearly the contrast in policies, ideas and ethos between the two parties. These differences go deep, as is indicated by the policy preferences of MPs on specific issues. The best substantial evidence of these differences dates from the 1960s and early 1970s, but is worth citing nonetheless in order to make the point. The first evidence derives from a study of the views of Conservative and Labour MPs on ten major issues in 1971. On five issues (comprehensive education, prices and incomes policy, trade union reform, foreign policy East of Suez and the principle of 'No independence before majority rule' in Rhodesia) the majority of Conservative MPs in the survey held opinions directly opposed to the majority of Labour MPs.[1] Differences between the parties

Table 3.1 *Party voting for reform on 'conscience' issues, 1964–68*

| | Labour | | Conservative | |
	For	Against	For	Against
Abolition of capital punishment	84·8	0·3	26·6	55·9
Homosexuality	50·8	9·1	20·2	27·3
Abortion	36·0	6·4	12·6	24·4
Divorce	43·9	5·7	9·2	33·2

Note: The figures refer to the percentage of each party which voted in a particular way, e.g. 84.8 per cent of the Labour Party voted for the abolition of capital punishment. Percentage figures 'for' and 'against' in each case do not total 100 as some Members were absent or abstained.

Source: Peter G. Richards, *Parliament and Conscience*, Allen and Unwin, 1970, p. 180

can be further illustrated from the way Conservative and Labour MPs voted on four 'conscience' issues in the 1960s. These votes are particularly interesting because the MPs were not subject to party pressures: they were free to vote as their consciences dictated. As Table 3.1 indicates, a majority of Labour MPs favoured liberalisation of the laws on divorce, abortion, homosexuality and capital punishment while most Conservatives opposed it.

When the House voted again on capital punishment in July 1979 and May 1982, on both occasions Labour voted nearly unanimously against its restoration and successively 68 per cent and 56 per cent of Conservatives voted to bring it back (see Table 3.2). The vote of July 14 1983 on the restoration of hanging confirmed this position. Labour opposed the return of capital punishment – this time with total unanimity; over two-thirds of Conservatives favoured its restoration.

The parties, then, differ profoundly. But their policies may also overlap. A sizeable minority of Conservatives supported the 'conscience' reforms. In 1975, an even larger minority of Labour MPs, amounting to well over one-third of the party, voted in

Table 3.2 *Party votes on capital punishment 1979 and 1982*

July 19, 1979. Motion: The sentence of capital punishment should again be available to the courts.

	For	Against	Did not vote	Total
Conservative	230	98	9	337
Labour	3	251	13	267
Liberal	2	9	0	11
Other	10	6	0	16
Totals*	245	364	22	631

	+Speaker and deputies	635

Majority: 119

May 11,1982. Motion: A person convicted of murder shall be liable to capital punishment

	For	Against	Did not vote	Total
Conservative	185	111	36	332
Labour	5	208	26	239
Liberal	1	9	2	12
SDP	0	25	4	29
Other	6	6	5	17
Totals*	197	359	73	629

	+Speaker and deputies	
	+2 seats vacant	635

Majority: 162   *Totals include tellers

Source: The Guardian, 13 May 1982

favour of joining the Common Market along with the vast majority of Conservatives. (See Table 3.3)

Again, there were several significant areas of common concern in the 1983 manifestos. Both parties pledged themselves to help first-time home-buyers, council tenants (especially with regard to their rights to repairs of their property) and pensioners. Both promised to ban lead in petrol. Finally, they demonstrated varying degrees of sympathy for animal welfare: the Conservatives promised to update the 1876 Cruelty to Animals Act to ensure

Table 3.3 *Party voting on the EEC, 9 April 1975*

	For	Against	Did not vote	Total
Labour				
Cabinet Ministers	14	7	0	21
Junior Ministers	31	31	9	71
Backbenchers	92	107	24	223
All Labour MPs	137	145	33	315
Conservative	249	8	18	275
Liberal	12	0	1	13
Scottish Nationalist	0	13	1	14
United Ulster Unionist	0	6	4	10
Others	0	0	2	2
Total	398	172	59	629

Source: D. Butler and U. Kitzinger, *The 1975 Referendum* (Macmillan, 1976), p. 52

the more humane treatment of laboratory animals; Labour committed itself to ban all hunting with dogs, including foxhunting, beagling and mink hunting.

There are a number of reasons for this overlap. Of course, there is always the possibility of intellectual agreement between people of similar background and education. But the parties are also exposed to similar circumstances and pressures. In social policy, for example, governments are pushed towards a consensus by pressure groups and the civil service, who give each party very similar advice, and by the inheritance of irreversible commitments from their predecessors. Moreover, the need to win votes compels each party to produce policies which will satisfy large sections of the electorate such as pensioners (7 million), owner-occupiers (11 million) and parents of dependent children (13 million). These form voting blocs which overlap class interests. Parties also face similar problems. In the mid-1970s, for instance, both parties in turn confronted the need to reduce the amount of teacher training because of the declining numbers of school-children; and both had to cope with an increasing proportion of old age pensioners in the total population, and with the decay of inner city areas.

Party groups, factions and tendencies

Both major parties are coalitions. Both contain groups which want to get their policies accepted by the party as a whole and to the extent that they succeed, the party may be said to have moved to the right or left, become more moderate or more extreme. These groups may be small or large; they may focus on one issue (alliances) or cover a wide range of policies; they may be transient or permanent; their operations may be limited to parliament or may extend throughout the party as a whole. They are of great importance to the two major parties.

Labour groups may be classified as 'right' or 'right-centre' and 'left', with the 'left' category further sub-divided into 'soft' and 'hard' (or 'outside') factions. The *Manifesto Group* was formed after the October 1974 general election to counter the influence of the Tribunite left. It rejects both unilateralism and withdrawal from the EEC and favours multilateralism and continuing membership of NATO as well as of the Common Market. It also fundamentally disagrees with the left wing of the Party over economic policy: whereas the left see the 'mixed economy' as a transitional stage on the way to complete state ownership, Labour Party moderates regard the mixed economy as good in itself. They consider a strong private sector to be vital both on grounds of economic efficiency and as a guarantee of political freedom. The Manifesto Group is revisionist – that is, its line of intellectual descent goes back to the attempt by Hugh Gaitskell (the party leader between 1955 and 1963) to 'revise' the party constitution away from its commitment to public ownership; they argue that revisionism has really succeeded but that the party cannot admit it. To the Manifesto Group, better management of the economy rather than more nationalisation is the best way to help the underprivileged.

In the early 1980s, the Group again became intensely concerned about the leftward drift of the party in general and about the adoption of members of the Militant tendency as Labour parliamentary candidates in particular. In the aftermath of the

1983 general election defeat, right-wingers drew attention to the need to modify 'extreme' policies in the light of the opinions of the general public and of their own supporters. Home ownership was popular and the party therefore should endorse it unequivocally. Despite hostility to Trident and Cruise, three-fifths of British people considered that the country was safer, rather than less safe, for possessing nuclear weapons. 77 per cent of the public and 64 per cent of Labour partisans thought that Britain should keep its nuclear weapons until other countries had been persuaded to reduce theirs; only 19 per cent and 33 per cent respectively considered that Britain should rid itself of nuclear weapons first, and *then* seek to persuade others to do the same.[2] Equally, in the view of right-wingers, party policy needed to move towards accepting this, too. Like Tribune, the Manifesto Group puts forward a 'slate' of its members for election to the Shadow Cabinet when Labour is in opposition. Leading Manifesto Group members who held Shadow Cabinet posts in 1984 included John Cunningham (Environment), Giles Radice (Education), Donald Dewar (Scotland) and Barry Jones (Wales).

Another group on the centre-right of the party is *Solidarity* (the Labour Solidarity Campaign). This group began in 1981 in opposition to the new procedure adopted by Labour for the election of its leader and deputy-leader by the Wembley conference. Moderate opinion in the party considered that the new electoral college method gave too much importance to the trade unions and to the constituency parties. 150 Labour MPs signed a statement opposing the decision, out of which Solidarity – 'the Gang of 150' – was born. It represented the riposte of the centre-right to the changes in the party constitution effected by the left. Roy Hattersley and Peter Shore took a leading part in forming it. But, although established to challenge the composition of the electoral college (40 per cent trade unions, 30 per cent Constituency Labour parties, 30 per cent Parliamentary Labour Party), it failed to mount an effective campaign to do so. Rather it concentrated on mobilising support behind Denis Healey for the deputy leadership.[3] After 1982, it devoted its efforts to excluding leading members of the Militant tendency from the party.

Roy Hattersley became deputy leader in 1983. With Neil Kinnock, he formed part of a combined centre-right/soft left 'ticket' for Labour's top jobs. Replacing Peter Shore as Shadow Chancellor in 1984, he immediately sought a viable alternative economic strategy to that of Conservative Government – one which would enable the country to avoid both the evils of high unemployment and high inflation. He called for moderate devaluation, limited import controls and an expansion in public sector borrowing to finance new public capital investment. Like previous Labour politicians on the centre-right of the party, he took issue with the trade unions on incomes and the left on nationalisation. A supporter of incomes policy, Hattersley had to persuade the unions, many of whom favoured free collective bargaining, that a formula on pay would enable a Labour Government to set far more ambitious goals for itself. On public ownership, he thought that traditional leftist calls for more nationalisation were outmoded and the dominant existing form of nationalisation unsuitable for present circumstances. In his view, a society in which a high percentage of productive capacity was owned by the State was unlikely to be highly efficient or truly free. Where public ownership was called for, Britain's industrial survival depended on developing new forms of public enterprise which would convince workers that British industry belonged to them by giving them a stake in their industries.[4]

Another group located on the centre-right of the Party is the *Fabian Society*, which was founded in 1884. Early members included Sidney and Beatrice Webb and George Bernard Shaw. Its founders thought that society was moving irresistibly towards the kind of socialism they supported and just needed to be given a push in the right direction. Their motto was 'the inevitability of gradualness'. The Fabians were one of several socialist groups which helped to form the Labour Party in 1900 and have been a fertile source of ideas and policies ever since. The 1975 Social Security Act, for example, which introduced superannuation for workers not included in occupational pension schemes, was largely based on ideas first proposed in a Fabian pamphlet in 1953. Its influence rests on the quality of the ideas proposed in its numerous publications rather than upon the size of its membership.

The most members it has ever had was 8,930 in 1972, but numbers have declined since then. However, Labour MPs usually join in large numbers, and, in 1984, about half the Parliamentary Labour Party (PLP) were members. The group was hard-hit in 1981 by the defection of leading Labour politicians to the SDP. All of the Gang of Four had been at some time on the Fabian executive, and two of them, Shirley Williams and Bill Rodgers, had been General Secretary of the society for a combined total of eleven years. The society decided by a ballot that people ineligible for Labour Party membership could not be full members of the Fabians. And the Gang of Four left, taking with them several hundred members including some large financial benefactors. However, the society had recovered from the worst effects of the exodus by 1984.

Situated on the 'soft left', the *Tribune Group* is one of the most important groups in the party. This left-wing faction was formed in 1965 by Michael Foot, Ian Mikardo and Stan Orme, but its intellectual origins may be traced to the Bevanites in the 1950s and even further back to the socialism of the Independent Labour Party. Its views are expressed in a weekly journal, *Tribune*, which was founded in 1937 by Stafford Cripps, Aneurin Bevan and George Strauss and whose present aim is stated by its editor, Richard Clements, to be 'the overthrow of capitalism and a rapid move towards Socialism'. In 1983 the group contained about seventy MPs, including Neil Kinnock, Brian Sedgemore, Eric Heffer and Renée Short. One source of embarrassment for the group between 1975 and 1979 was the presence of its former leader, Michael Foot, in the Cabinet, whose policies it strongly opposed. Its alternative economic strategy prescribed more nationalisation, the maintenance of high levels of public expenditure, state-directed investment through the National Enterprise Board, compulsory planning agreements with companies, and import and exchange controls. It has usually favoured import controls and been against incomes policies. It was opposed to Britain joining the Common Market and after five years of membership of the EEC considered that it had been a disaster for the country. In 1977 a pamphlet entitled *The Common Market: the costs of membership* was produced by the Tribunite Labour Common Market Safeguards Committee. It pointed out the adverse economic effects of membership and urged the party to oppose direct elections to the European Assembly, to seek an immediate and fundamental reform of the Common Agricultural Policy and to try to restore parliamentary control over ministerial decisions in Brussels and over Common Market rules.

After May 1982, when Chris Mullin became editor of *Tribune*, the relationship between the paper and the parliamentary group became troubled. Mullin swung *Tribune* from a Foot-ite to a Benn-ite position and declared the Tribune group of MPs to be dead. He was rebuked by Michael Foot for 'infantile leftism'. A board room dispute involving Mullin and John Silkin ended with Mullin's resignation. In July 1984, Neil Kinnock criticised *Tribune* for its stance on the reselection of MPs. The Labour leader wanted to introduce the possibility for CLPs (Constituency Labour parties) to ballot all their members on reselection whereas *Tribune* thought this would diminish the influence of the left. By late 1984, *Tribune* was attacking the leadership of Neil Kinnock and was aligning itself with the Campaign Group rather than with the parliamentary Tribunites, as formerly.

In the late 1970s, two groups emerged on the 'outside left' of the party, the Labour Coordinating Committee and the Campaign for Labour Party Democracy. Briefly, their aims were respectively: to commit the party to 'truly Socialist', i.e. left-wing objectives; and to ensure that these aims were carried out by changing the constitution to achieve greater accountability of the parliamentary leadership to the rank-and-file. The *Labour Coordinating Committee* (LCC) focused on policy issues such as withdrawal from the EEC, economic policy and press freedom, whilst the Campaign for Labour Party Democracy (CLPD) worked for changes in the party constitution. Unlike the Tribune Group, whose activities were confined to parliament, the LCC sought and gained grass-roots support, having about 800 members and between fifty and sixty affiliated organisations by 1981.[5] Leading members are Nigel Stanley, its first organising secretary, Peter Hain, the former Liberal and anti-Apartheid campaigner, and Hilary Barnard. Between 1980 and 1982, a broad umbrella organisation called the Rank and File Mobilising Committee was formed to exert maximum pressure for change. This brought together a variety of outside-left groups, which included the LCC, the CLPD, the Socialist Campaign for Labour Victory and the Trotskyist Militant tendency. Having radicalised the constitution and given the party a Socialist policy, the groups drew apart again in 1983. After the 1983 election, the LCC proposed an eleven-point plan for party unity on such matters as unilateralism, the minimum wage, reselection and women's rights. In late 1983, it moved doctrinally towards a 'soft left' position, accepting the inevitability of a mixed economy, albeit with only a small private sector. The LCC backed Neil Kinnock for the leadership, having supported Benn in 1979. Its political priorities in 1984–5 were as follows: to maintain trade union links to the Labour Party by winning the political funds ballots in the unions; and to encourage Labour local authorities to implement the party policy of non-compliance with rate-capping.[6]

The *Campaign for Labour Party Democracy* (CLPD) played the leading part in the campaign to change the Labour Party constitution in the late 1970s and early 1980s. Its fierce and effective fight to make Labour leaders and parliamentarians accountable to the whole party began in 1973. It originated in feelings of anger at the behaviour of the party under Harold Wilson, especially the flouting of a 'three-line whip' (particularly important pieces of parliamentary business are underlined three times) on the EEC vote by the pro-Marketeers (pp. 40–42) and the leader's veto on the party's nationalisation proposals before the February 1974 election. Its focus on the need for constitutional change derived from its conviction that without accountability all the policy resolutions in the world would come to nothing. But, in fact, the CLPD shared the ideology of other 'outside-left' groups: pro-large-scale public ownership, unilateral disarmament, withdrawal from the EEC and the removal of discrimination against women, blacks and other minorities. Its main constitutional objectives were a broader constituency within the party than the PLP for the election of leader; mandatory reselection of MPs; and final control over the manifesto by the NEC rather than the party leader. By 1981, the first two aims had been achieved, with momentous implications for both the party and British politics as a whole. For, had these changes not occurred, the Gang of Four would probably not have left the party to form the SDP and Neil Kinnock would probably not have been elected leader. The key figures of CLPD are both relatively unknown: Vladimir Derer, a Czech Socialist who fled to Britain in 1939, the principal organiser of the campaign; and Victor Schonfield, a jazz critic, who acted as a link with the trade unions, which play a central role in CLPD strategy. It has gained the support of leading hard left figures in the Labour Movement, including politicians like Joan Maynard, Jo Richardson and Audrey Wise and trade unionists such as Alan Sapper, General Secretary of ACTT and Bernard Dix of NUPE. Of all left politicians, however, Tony Benn was the closest to being the Group's figurehead, and it supported his campaign for the deputy-leadership in 1981. Its considerable success is also reflected in the fact that in 1980 it had over 800 individual members and 400 affiliated organisations, including 107 constituency Labour parties and 112 trade union branches. Persistent behind-the-scenes activity had brought the right-wing of the party into total disarray.

The *Campaign Group* is a well-organised hard left group, a breakaway from *Tribune*. The treasurer of this faction, which numbers over thirty MPs is Bob Clay, and Tony Benn, Max Madden, Dennis Canavan, Terry Fields and Dave Nellish attended the press conference to launch its pamphlet 'Parliamentary Democracy and the Labour Movement' in March 1984. This pamphlet proposed the subjection of all Crown prerogatives to the will of the House of Commons; the abolition of the House of Lords; restoration of control of all legislation to the House of Commons by the EEC; cancellation of agreements for US nuclear bases in the UK; the submission of all public appointments to the House of Commons for approval; and reforms of parliamentary procedure, including a reduction in the life of a parliament from five to four years. It favoured the election of a Labour Shadow Cabinet or Cabinet annually by an electoral college and also advocated that all future Labour Ministers should have teams of advisers elected by the specialist backbench committees. These ideas bore a similarity to the radicalism of Tony Benn, the leading figure on the party left in the early 1980s. Many members of this group made a demonstration in the House of Commons in November 1984 against proposed cuts in supplementary benefit for the families of striking miners. Disillusioned with Neil Kinnock at this time, the Campaign Group was considering challenging him for the leadership at the 1985 Bournemouth Conference.

The *Militant tendency* is a far left Trotskyist organisation whose existence within the party caused bitter dissension in the 1980s. Its ultimate objectives are set out in the pamphlet *Militant: What we stand for* (1981). They include the nationalisation of 200 monopolies, workers' control of the banks, a thirty-five hour week without reduction in earnings, a massive public works programme, withdrawal from the EEC and nuclear disarmament. But it is less its programme which provoked the furious reaction to it of the centre and right of the party, than its secret democratic centralist Leninist organisation and its contempt for parliamentary democracy. To Labour moderates, it was its organisational strength allied with its anti-democratic principles, rather than the fact that it was 'a party within a party', which made it a menace. The debate between right and left of the party over the issue of the Militant tendency's 'entryism' first erupted in 1977 over the appointment of Andy Bevan, a Trotskyist ex-Chairman of the Young Socialists, as the National Youth Officer of the party and developed into a series of hard-fought legal and procedural battles over the attempt to expel Militant after 1982. The difficulty for the party in taking action against Militant was increased by the abolition of the list of proscribed organisations in 1973 no less than by Militant's determination to resist expulsion and the shrewd tactics it employed in doing so. Its initial success in avoiding the consequences of expulsion (February 1983) was manifest in its ability to run five candidates in Labour colours at the 1983 election, two of whom, Dave Nellist (Coventry South-East) and Terry Fields (Liverpool Broadgreen) were elected. Even after the NEC confirmed the expulsion of the five members of its editorial board in July 1983, Militant continued to resist, until it seemed that the most effective if long-drawn-out way for the party to proceed was for its *constituency* parties to deal with Militant at the local level. In April 1984 the NEC voted 14–12 to uphold the Blackburn Labour Party's expulsion of six members of the Militant organisation. Later in the year, the NEC agreed to establish a working party to examine the nature and extent of the influence of Militant and other fringe groups in the party and to produce a document setting out the principles of democratic socialism. Militant would not go away. Indeed, by 1983, it was a very powerful organisation, with a membership of 4,700, an annual income of over £1 million and a staff of over 140 'full-timers'. This affluence rested not only upon the subscriptions and donations of its hard-pressed members, but also on the sales of its weekly newspaper, *Militant*, claimed at 40,000, but more probably about half that figure. Its tenacious survival owed most however, to the skilful leadership of Ted Grant, its theoretician, and Peter Taaffe, who is nominally the editor of *Militant* but who in practice functions more as General Secretary of the organisation. As well as its two parliamentary successes in 1983, the group was influential in certain trade unions (the small Bakers' Union, the Post Office Engineering Union and the civil service union, CPSU) and also on Merseyside, where it was the dominant faction on the Labour council.[7]

Other pressures for change within the party in the 1980s came from radical feminists and blacks. Radical feminists argued for free and integrated child care, equal pay and positive discrimination at work, a statutory minimum wage and action to restrict the sexist and degrading portrayal of women on the media. CLPD women demanded constitutional changes to advance the cause of women. These included the placing of a women on every parliamentary short-list; the election of women's sections (on the NEC and CLPD) by the women's conference (not the block vote); and the right to have five resolutions debated at Conference each year. But these demands were rejected by the 1984 Conference. Gwyneth Dunwoody criticised the CLPD women for failing to take more obvious steps to help women such as amongst other things battling to protect the social services, fighting for nursery education, and defending the 1967 Abortion Act. The 1984 Conference also rejected the request of blacks for the establishment of separate black sections in the party on the lines of the women's sections. As far as blacks were concerned, the undoubted importance of the votes of black people to the party had not been matched by increases in blacks' influence within the party either in terms of policies to benefit the black community or the adoption of blacks as parliamentary candidates. One suggested reason for the rejection of this demand was the fear that black sections might be taken over by the Militant tendency, just as the Young Socialists had been in the 1970s. But the issue was unlikely to disappear.

Conservative groups. In the twentieth-century there have been two major traditions within the Conservative Party: a progressive reforming tradition which favoured an expanded role for the state, and a libertarian tradition, stressing individual rights and freedoms and opposing collectivism. Sir Keith Joseph and his supporters fit into the system of ideas which the Conservative Party inherited from nineteenth-century liberalism of doctrinaire support for free enterprise capitalism and outright hostility to the socialist planned economy. By contrast, the *Tory Reform Group*, whose leading spokesman is Peter Walker, is more sympathetic to government intervention in the economy and industry and less convinced of the value of the 'free' market. Tory Reformers tend to support the record of the 1970–74 Heath Government – notably its statutory incomes policy and its aid to ailing firms.

Sir Keith Joseph has attributed Britain's economic problems to a combination of government interference, high taxation, erosion of incentives and a variety of trade union practices: 'We are over-governed, over-spent, over-taxed, over-borrowed and over-manned.'[8] His solution is a monetarist economic policy and a large-scale reduction of the public sector. He is opposed to any form of 'social contract' – government concessions to the unions in return for voluntary wage restraint – as 'the root cause of the inflation, unemployment, stagnation, and balance of payments crises which have plagued us over the last two years'. In fact, he dislikes all forms of incomes policy. He also opposes government aid to firms in difficulties such as British Leyland because in his view it simply creates concealed unemployment. Sir Keith's ideal is the 'social market economy', in which shareholder and con-sumer choose freely in the market to ensure the most efficient allocation of goods and services. The only alternative, he has contended, is a command economy which, in turn, means 'a command society', in which the state increasingly dominates social life. Only the social market economy can ensure economic and political freedom. Nor need such an economy involve the neglect of the poor and underprivileged: indeed, the greater wealth produced by an efficient and successful private sector will enable even better provision to be made for these groups.

After 1974, these views were propounded by the *Centre for Policy Studies*. The Centre was established by Margaret Thatcher and Sir Keith to compare British and European economic experience and to examine the scope for introducing social market policies. It now works to popularise economic liberalism amongst party activists as well as to assist Sir Keith with research for his speeches. In addition to Sir Keith's own pamphlets, its publications include *Why Britain needs a market economy* (1975). In a memorandum of March 1983, it recommended legislation to prohibit strikes in essential services, such as ambulance, fire, gas, water, electricity and hospital nursing. Workers who were forbidden to strike should enjoy statutory improvements in pay and conditions in order to keep up with other industries and services. There should be compulsory arbitration procedures for settling disputes and substantial fines and imprisonment for strikers where death or serious injury to members of the public resulted from their actions. Sir Alfred Sherman, an adviser to Mrs Thatcher and *Daily Telegraph* leader writer, was its chairman down to 1983. When he left on a year's sabbatical, Lord Hugh Thomas, the historian, a strong advocate of free enterprise, free trade within the Common Market and national self-renewal, took over. The *Institute for Economic Affairs* (IEA) also propagates economic liberalism, but to a largely academic readership. This right-wing body became very influential under the premiership of Mrs Thatcher and a useful guide to ideas that were being discussed in government circles. In a pamphlet published under the auspices of the IEA in April 1984, Professor Patrick Minford of Liverpool University called for a massive programme of privatisation, including railways, coal, hospitals, schools and the Forestry Commission. He also recommended the abolition of the Manpower Services Commission, the Advisory, Concilation and Arbitration Service (ACAS) and large cuts in government support to agriculture. In his view, such measures would enable the government to cut taxes, treble child benefits, abolish National Insurance contributions, and reduce VAT by 4 per cent. Output would rise by 10 per cent and employment by 2·5 million.[9]

Another stronghold of libertarian Conservatism is the *Selsdon Group*. It was formed in 1973 and was a consequence of the disappointment felt by some Conservatives at the failure of the Heath Government to carry out the policies contained in the 1970 manifesto and first adopted by the Conservative Shadow Cabinet at Selsdon Park just before the 1970 general election. In 1975 its editorial director, Philip Vander Elst, called for a dismantling of the 'universalist welfare state' and denationalisation. He argued that the state should lay down and enforce minimum standards in health and education but that the actual provision of these services should be given over to private agencies. Public corporations should be denationalised or, failing this, private companies should be allowed to compete with them. In this way, consumer choice and economic efficiency would be enhanced and many more people would acquire a vested interest in the success of the market economy by becoming shareholders.[10] In its *Second Selsdon Group Manifesto* (1977), the group anticipated many of the characteristic themes of Conservative Governments after 1979. It argued that government should run the economy on a more market-orientated basis, control inflation by keeping a tight grip on money supply, privatise national assets as far as practicable, reduce public sector expenditure as a percentage of Gross National Product (GNP), abolish exchange controls, weaken the monopoly power of the unions, encourage private and voluntary initiatives in health, education and welfare, exclude the CBI and the TUC from economic policy-making, attack quangos and use the tax system to reinforce inequality. This meant an end to government intervention with regard to prices, wages and dividend controls, regional policies, industrial training and job creation schemes, employment subsidies and investment grants and incentives. It wanted the nationalised industries to be reintegrated into the private sector by restructuring their ownership and forcing them to raise funds on the private market. At the 1983 Conservative Conference, in an address to the group, Rhodes Boyson described unlimited government as a danger to the West and proposed reduced taxes, the break-up of nationalised industries and deregulation to create a genuinely competitive economy as the best remedy.

In short, the Selsdon Group is a 'free market' pressure group, the leading proponent of economic liberalism. It believes that the basic principle on which Conservative policies should rest is that public wants should be provided by the market and paid for by the people as consumers rather than as taxpayers. The task of government should not be to provide services but to maintain the framework within which markets operate. It is convinced that political freedom depends upon and is impossible without economic freedom. Under the governments of Mrs Thatcher, it has seen its role as twofold: first, to support the policies of the government when attacked, and to discourage reversals; and second, to encourage the government to carry out its monetarist policies with even greater rigour. In 1980, its 250 members included seven MPs.[11]

Unlike the Selsdon Group, which has concentrated upon drawing a small committed membership, the *Monday Club* has sought a mass membership amongst Conservative supporters. Another right-wing group, it was formed in 1961 to reassert true Conservative principles at the grass-roots level by Tories who considered that the party under Macmillan had shifted too far to the left. In particular, its founders disliked the argument of Macmillan's 'winds of change' speech that white supremacy in South Africa must end and the group has continued to express strongly right-wing views on questions of race ever since. In the 1960s, as well as emphasising the dangers of Soviet expansionism and advocating a strong defence establishment, the group gave vehement support to the Rhodesian and South African regimes. Its particular concerns have been the menace of international communism, declining moral standards, law and order, and 'socialism', which it equates with bureaucratic controls and inefficiency. Its views on economic policy and the welfare state are close to those of the Selsdon Group. Its journal, *Monday World*, styles itself 'the magazine of the Radical Right'. The club is a vociferous champion of the views of local activists, whom it sees as neglected, but its impact has been diminished by its lack of a frontbench spokesman of real stature. In 1971–2, its Immigration Committee under the chairmanship of George Kennedy Young (later chairman of the even more extreme *Tory Action*), developed close links with the extreme right. But the club was divided on British entry to the Common Market in 1972, and support for it declined. In 1984, it had 2000 members, including eighteen MPs and fifteen peers.

The club has continued to express strong opinions on matters of race and immigration. In October 1984, a black member, Derek Laud, in a paper entitled '*The Law, Order and Race Relations*', maintained that racial tension was being aggravated by the attempts of successive governments to bring into being a multi-racial society. He called for the abolition of the Commission for Racial Equality. The club advocates a ban on all further immigration and thinks that generous resettlement provisions should be offered to those who wish to take advantage of them. In March 1984, its political adviser, John Piniger, and three other members resigned in controversial circumstances, complaining of infiltration by extremists. But members of the club riposted by pointing out that Piniger had co-authored three publications on immigration, one of which had recommended an improved repatriation scheme for New Commonwealth and Pakistani immigrants who wished to leave. Clearly, just another factional struggle was taking place.

One motive for the formation of the Monday Club was to counter the influence of the Bow Group, which at that time was on the left of the party. The *Bow Group* was founded in 1951 to develop non-Socialist political ideas. Rather like the Fabians, it seeks to be non-partisan, or rather less partisan than other groups, simply publishing papers to stimulate discussion. It has remained primarily a London-based research group aiming to influence Conservative policy through its pamphlets and quarterly magazine, *Crossbow*. Typically, the Bow Group has provided a platform for Young Conservative intellectuals on the progressive wing of the party. Membership (1,000 in 1975) is open to all Conservatives, but the group does not express a collective view nor does it organise meetings within the parliamentary party. Its independent stance means that Bow Group pamphlets may lean towards either of the two ideological tendencies in the party. *A Chancellor's Primer*, for example, published by its Economic Affairs Standing Committee, reflected the views of the libertarian Right whereas *A Primrose Path? Tory attitudes to Social reform*, by Nicholas Scott, published at the same time, expressed the 'one nation' approach associated with Heath and Macmillan. However, during the period when the Conservatives were in opposition after 1975, the group moved towards the right of the party, expressing support for monetary economics and appealing for a greater sense of national purpose.

The Bow Group, which numbered ninety MPs and seven government Ministers among its members in 1983, has become a right of centre group. An article in *Crossbow* on the eve of the Conservative Conference in 1983 attacked the government for not being sufficiently radical either in its economic policy or in its approach to the welfare state. It advocated stimulating the economy by large-scale public investment schemes such as the electrification of the railways (possibly with private finance) together with a radical revision of policies towards the welfare state to take account of low economic growth. In 1984, the group was even more outspoken in its criticism of the government. In an open letter to the Prime Minister, its chairman, Michael Lingens, described the government's second term of office to that date as 'a dismal record of missed opportunities'. He urged the government to make tax cuts, reduce public expenditure, widen share ownership, reform the tax and social security system and revise its policies on environmental protection.

The *Salisbury Group* is a political society formed in 1978 by Roger Scruton and other academics. It aims to advance Conservatism intellectually as a precondition of creating a more favourable climate of opinion in general. It publishes the *Salisbury Review* which has a small circulation of about 1,000 (in 1983) but is widely read in government circles. It attacks influential Liberals and Socialists in the United States and England such as Noam Chomsky, Ronald Dworkin and E. P. Thompson. In particular, it has sought to undermine the post-1945 '*Guardian*-reader' orthodoxy of the liberal-left.

The *Tory Reform Group* represents a more 'moderate' vein within Conservative thinking. Established in 1975, it incorporates three earlier groups on the left or progressive reforming wing of the Party – Pressure for Economic and Social Toryism (PEST), the Social Tory Action Group and the Macleod Group. It represents the Disraelian 'one nation' tradition of Conservative thinking and is concerned about the social divisiveness of Mrs Thatcher's rhetoric and the government's monetarist policies.

One problem for the group has been that its most influential member, Peter Walker, is a member of the Cabinet. However, during 1983–4, with the unemployment figures remaining obdurately high, Walker made repeated veiled criticisms of government policy, culminating in a comprehensive repudiation of monetarism in the Harold Macmillan Lecture in November 1984. He endorsed Macmillan's 'middle way' policy of searching for an accommodation between the competing claims of capital and labour and defended the consensus politics of 1945–1970 as a period of low unemployment, high growth and the lowest inflation rates in British history. The previous month, in a speech to the Reform Group, he argued that Britain needed to assist its industries in the way that Germany and Japan assisted theirs and maintained that public expenditure could save industry as in the case of British Leyland, rather than undermine it. These speeches typify Reform Group attitudes. After 1979, for example, it agreed with Sir Geoffrey Howe on the need to reduce the top rates of income tax, to lower interest rates and to introduce tax credit and profit-sharing schemes. However, the Group does advocate a statutory incomes policy, ruling out the possibility of a voluntary agreement with the trade unions; in particular, if favours strict government control of wages in the public sector. Its incomes policy would discriminate in favour of workers in manufacturing industry. Similarly, the attitude of the group to public expenditure is considerably more flexible than that of Sir Keith Joseph: it distinguishes between public expenditure which raises productivity (such as investment in the coal, steel and aerospace industries) from that which is irrelevant to economic recovery. Whereas Sir Keith Joseph thinks that the inner-city areas can be revived by the restoration of incentives to businessmen and the elimination of bureaucratic planning procedures, Peter Walker has proposed a large programme of government investment and housing in these areas and a special emphasis on the creation of jobs.

As well as statutory wage restraint and profit sharing, the group has also supported industrial partnership, devolution and electoral reform. In October 1984, a pamphlet written by its chairman, Rodney Gent, argued against the abolition of the

GLC. It publishes its own journal, *Reformer*, and had thirty-five backbench supporters in 1984, a considerable reduction on the eighty it had in 1978. It has a grass-roots existence and had about 1,000 members in 1979. It has the support of the Young Conservatives, the Federation of Conservative Students, parts of Central Office and the Conservative Trade Unionists. The *Conservative Trade Unionists* organisation (CTU) have been likened to 'blue moles' burrowing away in the unions. It has three full-time regional officials (in Scotland, Yorkshire and the North-West), a National Director, four staff in London and the backing of Central Office. During the miners' strike, it was said to be influential in back-to-work miners' groups in several areas, notably Yorkshire.

On a broad range of issues, then, encompassing incomes policy, public expenditure, regional policy, industrial relations, workers' participation and devolution, the left- and right-wings of the Conservative Party disagreed with each other in the late 1970s and early 1980s. In terms both of numerical strength and political influence however, the moderates or 'wets' were a declining force. The right-wing or 'dry' side of the party enjoyed a powerful supremacy both in Cabinet and in parliament. Either as a result of sacking (Norman St. John Stevas, Ian Gilmour and Francis Pym) or resignation (Jim Prior), the 'wets' lacked influence in government. But together with Edward Heath, who had never been a member of the Thatcher Government, they possessed powerful potential as critics even if they did seem reluctant to realise this potential by acting in concert.

Like the Labour Party, the Conservatives have experienced problems of infiltration – or 'entryism' – by extremist groups and organisations in the 1970s and 1980s. A secret internal report by a committee of Young Conservatives in 1983 named four Conservative MPs who had had contacts with racialist or neo-fascist groups, and three Tory MPs elected in 1983, three Conservative councillors and four Conservative council candidates who had past associations with extreme right-wing groups. The report provided an insight into the activities of groups and organisations which served as channels of extremist influence either within the party like the Monday Club (described as 'an important channel for racist sentiments') or linking Conservative MPs with extreme right-wing opinion such as *WISE* (Welsh, Irish, Scottish, English) and *Tory Action*.[†]

It suggested that the Prime Minister had not done enough to combat racialism within the party and made a number of recommendations to combat extreme right activities within the party. These included denying such groups as WISE and Tory Action the use of Central Office premises; drawing up a proscribed list of Conservative Party candidates; requiring that local parties should ask all potential candidates whether they had been members of other political organisations; and establishing a standing committee to monitor collaboration and infiltration. The party banned the extremist coordinating groups from the use of Central Office facilities and early in 1984 was discussing tightening up its procedures for the approval of parliamentary candidates so that they would be automatically required to state whether they had ever belonged to any other political party.[12] But John Selwyn Gummer, the party chairman, considered it improbable that the party would set up a unit to monitor infiltration. He personally did not think there was evidence of significant infiltration into the party.[‡]

[†] The aims of WISE are 'to encourage the sense of kinship with our own people', to protect the interests of the 'indigenous peoples of these islands' and to promote 'the quite realistic repatriation of post-war immigrants to their own homelands'. According to the YC Report, its function is to organise meetings to bring together Tory MPs and extreme racialist groups. The function of *Tory Action*, according to its chairman, J. K. Young, is to strengthen party attitudes on such issues as law and order, race and immigration. He claims the Group keeps in touch with about twenty-four MPs. It also maintains a network of correspondents in about 100 local Conservative Associations. Its newsletter, according to the Report, has used openly racialist language and advocated repatriation.

[‡] The published version of the Young Conservatives Report consisted of ten pages only whereas the original draft was thirty-six pages long. Much had been omitted including four chapters documenting the infiltration entitled 'The Evidence Today'.

Party organisation at Westminster and outside

Choice of leaders. How the Labour and Conservative parties choose their leaders is of great importance because they are in effect choosing a likely Prime Minister. Leadership contests are therefore dramatic and exciting affairs, with parties, media and public all aware of the vital consequences of their outcomes.

Methods of election differ. The procedure of the Conservatives dates from 1965: previously, their leaders were not elected but rather 'emerged' from a complex and secretive process of taking soundings of party opinion. Under the present system, for a candidate to succeed on the first ballot, he or she must have an absolute majority of the votes cast plus a 15 per cent lead over the nearest rival. If he or she fails to secure this, nominations take place again and may include candidates who did not take part in the first ballot. In the second round an absolute majority of the votes cast is enough to secure victory; a third (and final) ballot, restricted to the three leading candidates may be held if the second ballot fails to produce a clear verdict. This time the single alternative vote is used, by which MPs also register their second preferences. If their first preferences still do not produce an overall winner, the candidate with the least first preferences is eliminated and the second preferences of those voting for this candidate are distributed between the two leading contenders until a winner appears. Recent leadership contests provide a chance to study the system in action.

In 1965, when these rules were employed for the first time, one ballot was sufficient because, although Edward Heath (150) lacked a 15 per cent majority over Reginald Maudling (133) and Enoch Powell (15), his two rivals withdrew from the contest and a second ballot was unnecessary. Ten years later, two ballots were required. Mrs Margaret Thatcher (130) won the first round against Edward Heath (119) and Hugh Fraser (16), but failed to achieve the necessary 15 per cent lead. Heath withdrew and, in the second ballot, Mrs Thatcher (146) did gain the necessary absolute majority over the other candidates, William Whitelaw (79), James Prior (19), Sir Geoffrey Howe (19) and John Peyton (11).

Before 1981, to win the leadership of the Labour Party, a

candidate had to secure a majority of the votes cast by the Parliamentary Labour Party (PLP). The present method dates from the decision of a Special Conference held at Wembley on 24 January 1981. The party constitution now requires both the leader and deputy leader to be chosen by an electoral college in which affiliated trade unions have 40 per cent of the votes and the PLP and Constituency Labour Parties (CLPs) 30 per cent each. If there is no overall winner after the first ballot, the candidate with the fewest votes drops out and a second ballot is held. Voting is open, not secret as in the previous system. The new procedure was first employed in the deputy leadership election of 1981. Votes were cast as follows: first ballot – Denis Healey 45·5 per cent, Tony Benn 36·6 per cent, John Silkin 18 per cent. Silkin was eliminated and in the second ballot Healey won by an extremely narrow margin: Healey 50·43 per cent, Benn 49·57 per cent. Benn triumphed in the constituency parties by a large majority (4:1 ratio) but Healey just won the unions (3:2) and more easily in the PLP (nearly 2:1).[13]

In 1983, Neil Kinnock won the leadership and Roy Hattersley the deputy leadership decisively on the first ballot. Voting for the leader was as follows: Neil Kinnock 71·3 per cent, Roy Hattersley 19·3 per cent, Eric Heffer 6·3 per cent and Peter Shore 3·1 per cent. Neil Kinnock won the vast majority of votes in the CLPs, almost three-quarters of the trade unions and nearly half the PLP. In the election for deputy leader. Roy Hattersley (67·3 per cent) comfortably outdistanced his rivals Michael Meacher (27·9 per cent), Denzil Davies (3·5 per cent) and Gwyneth Dunwoody (1·3 per cent); unlike their Conservative counterparts Labour leaders can be challenged in any year, both when the party is in opposition and when it is in government.[14]

Differing views on leadership election methods reflect political divisions within the parties. Present Conservative procedures resulted from the serious dissatisfaction within the Party with the way Sir Alec Douglas-Home had 'emerged' as leader in 1963. Rules enabling an existing leader to be challenged were adopted in 1975 because of discontent with the leadership of Edward Heath, who had lost three of the four general elections he had fought. In 1980–1, both the right and the left of the Labour Party wanted to give more say to the party outside parliament in the election of the leader and deputy leader. But they differed profoundly on where the preponderance of power should lie. Having decided in principle in favour of a wider franchise for the leadership elections, the 1980 party conference left the all-important details of how this should be done to be worked out by a Special Rules Revision Conference (Wembley 1981), at which the unions wielded nearly 90 per cent of the votes. The decision was made in two stages, at each of which the 'moderate' or right wing of the party lost. The first decision was whether the vote should be by individual members of the party (i.e. excluding members affiliated by the trade unions) or by some form of electoral college. The Conference decided by a huge majority in favour of an electoral college at annual conference, a proposition which received over 6·25 million votes to the mere 431,000 for election by ballot of individual members. The second main decision concerned the allocation of 'weightings' to the different sections of the party represented in the electoral college. Three schemes were put forward: PLP, Trade Unions, CLPs 33 per cent each (with affiliated societies 1 per cent); trade unions 40 per cent, PLP and CLPs 30 per cent each; and PLP 50 per cent and trade unions and CLPs 25 per cent. Broadly, the right wanted most proportionate weight to be given to the PLP, the left wanted the balance of advantage to favour the constituency parties and the trade unions. Once again the left may be said to have triumphed since the scheme adopted (trade unions 40 per cent, PLP and CLPs 30 per cent each) gave a higher proportionate weighting to the trade unions and CLPs than either of the other two schemes. The party structure on this issue had been federalised rather than democratised.

Lastly, the elections of leaders provide another occasion for factional struggles within the parties. The 1983 Labour leadership contest was widely seen as a struggle between the centre-left of the party (Neil Kinnock) and the centre-right (Roy Hattersley) and the struggle for the deputy leadership as being between the centre-right (Hattersley) and hard left (Michael Meacher). When Kinnock and Hattersley respectively won, this was widely reported as a victory for the 'dream ticket' since it helped to unite both wings of the party.

Whips and party cohesion. One of the most important tasks of the party leader is to hold the party together. The competing individuals, groups and interests within the two major parties make this a difficult job. If the party splits, it is almost certain to suffer electoral defeat. The 1975 Referendum showed the lengths to which a party leader will go to preserve party unity. Both the decision to hold the referendum itself and the fact that Cabinet Ministers were allowed to differ from official government policy in the country (although not in parliament) testified to the intensity of the Labour leader's resolve to hold the party together. In this task, any party leader has certain advantages. The desire of ambitious politicians to gain governmental office makes them anxious to remain in favour. At all times they will try to avoid giving aid or comfort to the other party: there is a natural desire, therefore, to avoid abstention or cross-voting. This wish is reinforced by conviction; very many of them joined the party for a purpose and out of a belief in its objectives. There is also the more self-interested concern to keep their local party happy; constituency organisations have powers to 'hire and fire' and generally dislike rebellions against party policy.

It is therefore largely in the formal sense that party discipline is the responsibility of the Whips. MPs actually vote with their parties for a great many reasons other than the formal powers of the Whips, and the Whips themselves are aware of the practical limits of their demands. As Bob Mellish (who was Labour Chief Whip in the late 1960s) said in response to a question about what he did when someone voted against the party line: 'Well, first of all I get upset and then after that I have to live with it.'[15] Withdrawal of the Whip may be an effective threat against one or two individuals but thirty MPs can hardly be expelled from the party.

Nonetheless, the Whips play a vital role in the organisation of contemporary parliamentary parties. They are more concerned with providing their leaders with information about party opinion than with enforcing discipline. Their job is to anticipate and to avoid possible ruptures through consultation rather than to take action once they have occurred. Their main administrative task is to organise the party vote in parliament. Each week they produce and send to MPs the documentary Whip – an outline of parliamentary business which indicates the degrees of importance attached by the party to the various items. Particularly important items are underlined three times. A Member's attendance for such business is essential and defiance of a 'three line whip' is a serious offence. Less important matters are underlined twice, minor ones once only. The consent of the Chief Whip is necessary for pairing – the arrangement by which an MP of one party can miss a vote provided he can find someone on the other side who will also stay away. In the Conservative Party the leader appoints the Chief Whip and decides whether to withdraw the Whip from a particular MP; in the Labour Party, these functions are carried out by the PLP.

Party committees. There are three types of party committee at Westminster: the whole parliamentary party, specialist policy committees and the Shadow Cabinet. The Conservative Party meets as a body in the *1922 Committee* (the Conservative Private Members' Committee) and the Labour Party as the PLP (Parliamentary Labour Party). The Conservative Leader does not attend the 1922 Committee when the party is in opposition but does so as Prime Minister. When the Labour Party is in office a Liaison Committee is elected. This consists of a minority of ministers and a majority of backbenchers, its role being to maintain contacts between the Cabinet and backbench MPs. Exchanges of opinion in these important committees are franker and often fiercer than in the Commons itself, as leaders seek to persuade backbenchers of the wisdom of their policies and tactics.

Both parties also form a large number of specialist committees, where backbenchers can discuss policy among themselves and with frontbenchers. In 1973, there were thirty-one Conservative sub-committees and forty-seven policy groups of the PLP. When the party is in opposition, Conservative committees are chaired by the appropriate Shadow Minister; when the party is in power, by backbenchers. Labour arrangements are similar, although in opposition the chairmen are necessarily drawn from the Shadow Cabinet. Labour's groups can make policy proposals, which are then referred to a full meeting of the PLP. Both parties also have regional groups bringing together MPs for particular localities (e.g. Greater London, Scotland, North East England).

Each major party in opposition selects a Shadow Cabinet. In the Conservative Party the leader chooses this group, which is usually referred to as the Consultative Committee. In the Labour Party the Shadow Cabinet is based on the Parliamentary Committee elected annually by the PLP, although the leader does allocate specific portfolios. Thus, Labour's Shadow Cabinet consists of the Parliamentary Committee of fifteen members together with several *ex officio* members: the leader himself, the deputy-leader, the elected chairman of the backbench MPs, the leader of the Party in the House of Lords, the Chief Whip in the Lords, and an elected representative of backbench peers. The voting in Labour Shadow Cabinet elections regularly reflects the left-right divisions within the party, although not exclusively so. Some MPs always attract votes simply for doing a good job and steering clear of controversy. In addition, the Labour leader appoints assistants for each Shadow Minister; in 1984 the entire Shadow Cabinet contained sixty-two members.

Outside Westminster, parties exist at a number of levels. First, there are the ordinary members who participate little in party affairs beyond the payment of a subscription and attendance at the occasional meeting. Then there are the more active members who are involved in canvassing, letter-writing and serving on committees. Finally, there are the paid professional workers in the party organisation, whether in the central, regional or constituency offices. This section deals with the party organisations in the country and with their relationships with their parliamentary parties.

The major parties are very different in character but, in one important respect at least, they do resemble one another. Surveys have repeatedly shown that the views of party activists are more 'extreme' than the prevailing views inside the parliamentary parties. Constituency Labour parties and extra-parliamentary groups are to the left of most Labour MPs, whereas the opinions of Conservative Party activists are generally to the right of the parliamentary party. The relationship between the political views of voters, parliamentary parties and party activists may be expressed as follows:[16]

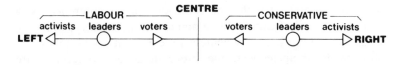

This situation is of the greatest importance in British politics. It means that both party leaders are under constant pressure from their closest supporters outside parliament to adopt more 'extreme' positions, while at the same time, in the interests of electoral victory, they must appeal to the political centre where the majority of voters are to be found. Party leadership, therefore, is a delicate balancing act and much of British government turns on the success with which it is performed.

Outside Westminster, the ethos of the Labour Party is egalitarian, working-class and broadly socialist; the Conservative Party is hierarchical, middle-class and capitalist. A glance at their histories helps to explain much about the contrasting character of the two party organisations. The Labour Party is in origin a mass movement. The aim of the trade unions and socialist societies which formed the Labour Representation Committee (1900) was to get more working men into parliament. Its ideals were democratic and 'labourist' but not, until 1918, socialist; leaders were elected by their supporters and were expected to be accountable to them. The parliamentary party was a later (1906) extension of this mass movement, which stressed the primary importance of rank-and-file members.

The National Union of Conservative and Constitutional Associations began in 1867 at a meeting called, in the aftermath of the Second Reform Act, to consider ways of making Conservative principles 'effective among the masses'. Its main purpose was to organise new associations and to co-ordinate the activities of existing ones.[17] Local parties thus emerged as servants of the party in parliament rather than the other way round. The leading function of the National Union is to convene an Annual Conference of constituency associations in order 'to promote the circulation of opinion between them and the leaders of the party'. Representatives from the constituency associations at Conference heavily outnumber those from the Young Conservatives, Conservative trade unionists and women's organisations, and permanent officers. To the party leadership, Conference is a sounding-board of Conservative opinion in the country, while the rank-and-file are normally content to leave matters of policy and strategy to their leaders; the proceedings of Conference are usually uncontroversial, with resolutions often passed without a vote. It was not until the mid-1960s that the leader began to attend the whole Conference; before that, he went only on the final day.

In contrast to this unitary structure, power in the Labour Party is constitutionally dispersed among a number of sources. Trade union influence goes back to the beginning: two-thirds of the members of the Labour Representation Committee in 1900 were trade unionists. The trade unions provide over two-thirds of the party's income, over five-sixths of its membership and play a dominant role at Conference: their power lies in their Conference votes. Affiliated membership in the party (through unions, co-operative societies and socialist societies) is over 5 million – that is, over ten times as large as individual membership (in consti-tuency parties). Votes are allocated to unions in proportion to the annual sum which they pay as an affiliation fee and each union casts its votes as a block vote which is not divided up according to any differences of opinion among the membership. In practice, delegates from the constituency parties usually out-number union delegates at Conference but the combined block votes of the five largest unions can normally command an ab-solute majority.

According to the constitution (adopted in 1918), Conference is the ruling body of the Labour Party and the National Executive Committee (NEC) manages the party between Conferences. Members of the NEC are elected annually by Conference as follows: twelve by the unions, seven by the constituency parties, five women's representatives and one each from the Cooperative Movement, the socialist societies and the Young Socialists; the leader and deputy-leader are *ex officio* members. Conference decides which proposals to include in the party programme but this is only a guide to the party manifesto. The final decision about what goes into the manifesto is, constitutionally, the joint responsibility of the Parliamentary Committee of the PLP and the National Executive Committee, or, when the party is in office, of the Cabinet and the NEC. The presence of the leader and deputy-leader on both the Parliamentary Committee and the NEC helps to defuse conflict between the moderate parliamentary and left-wing extra-parliamentary sections of the party. The leader's position also gives him greater authority than the Chairman of the NEC, who was originally intended to be his equal. Policy-formation, then, is a matter of agreement between the various sections of the party, with the leader requested to perform a delicate balancing act. In 1972, the formation of the Liaison Committee, to which the PLP, the NEC and the TUC contributed their three most senior members, gave institutional recognition to the need for compromise. But, as opinion inside it veered to the left, the party became very difficult to control in the 1970s, and nearly split over the EEC. In 1979, in the wake of the election defeat, controversy broke out again over the party constitution. Left wingers wanted to make the NEC alone responsible for the party manifesto but moderates successfully resisted such a change.

Authority in the Conservative Party is concentrated in the leadership. The leader appoints the Chairman of Central Office and, in consultation with his closest colleagues, decides upon policy. Yet the strong influences of autocracy in the Conservative Party and of democracy in the Labour Party are both modified in practice. In fact, Conservative leaders have been less secure than Labour leaders in the twentieth century. Moreover, they always need to listen carefully to what the different sections of the party are saying. The federalistic Labour Party is more difficult to handle as events in the early 1980s blatantly demonstrated. But normally its desire for office puts powerful weapons in the hands of the leader. Both parties are easier to lead in government than in opposition.

The party civil services
Neither of the major parties could survive for long without the services of a large number of full-time officials – administrators, agents, publicists and researchers – for many of whom party work is a permanent career. Their tasks are to raise money, help to run election campaigns, assist in the selection of parliamentary candidates, conduct research, promote political education and re-

cruit party workers. Liaison with the other two main elements in each party organisation – the parliamentary party and its institutions outside Westminster – is a vital part of the work of these officials of Central Office (Conservative) and Transport House (Labour) and of their countrywide staffs.

Overall responsibility for Conservative organisation lies with the Chairman of the Party although day-to-day administration is done by the Deputy Chairman. The leading official of the Labour Party, the General Secretary, is appointed by the National Executive Committee. Conservative Central Office has three departments: Organisation, Research and Publicity; Transport House has Information, International and Research departments and its National Agent is also a departmental head. Research staff are the largest single group at both party headquarters.

The key professional workers in both parties, and the most numerous, are the local agents. Agents link the parties' central headquarters with their regional, area and constituency bodies, and also play an important role in fund-raising. Agents are certificated, trained and promoted by the central organisations, although normally they are employed by the constituency parties. Since 1969, however, both parties have established National Agency Services, so that they can draft agents into crucial marginal seats, and these services are run by the central party headquarters. The Conservative Party employs far more agents than Labour, but in both parties their numbers have decreased markedly since 1945.

Each party maintains contact with the constituencies through a network of Area (Conservative) or Regional (Labour) offices. The senior area official acts as secretary to the Area or Regional Councils, thereby providing a link between the parties' central organisations and their constituency parties. The Area and Regional Councils form the middle tier of the *representative* side of each party organisation between the constituency parties and the national conference. Each party's Area or Regional office supervises about fifty constituencies.

Conservative constituency associations are run by Executive Councils composed of representatives of ward or district branches, Young Conservatives, Conservative Clubs and other coopted members. The General Management Committees which run Constituency Labour Parties reflect the federal structure of the Party and are composed of delegates from trade union branches, socialist and cooperative societies and local Labour parties. However, most of the actual business is done by smaller committees: by the General Purposes Committees on behalf of the Executive Councils of Conservative Associations and by Executive Committees for the General Management Committees of Constituency Labour Parties. Constituency parties canvass, keep registers of voters' intentions, raise funds and provide transport to the polls on election days. But their most important function is to select party candidates for parliament.

The selection of parliamentary candidates
The way in which parties select candidates for parliament is of vital significance. In Britain, two-thirds of constituencies are 'safe' seats for one party or another and to be adopted by the majority party in one of these is to be virtually certain of election to parliament. But, before ordinary voters go to the polls, local parties choose the candidates.

Whereas the conduct of elections is closely regulated by law, the parties themselves decide the procedure for candidate selection. Constitutionally, in both parties, this process is closely supervised by the central organisations. The Conservative Party maintains a list of approved candidates. Before 1981, the Vice-Chairman responsible for candidates had the task of vetting candidates for this list. In 1981, however, the system changed. Would-be parliamentary candidates were prompted into going before residential Parliamentary Selection Boards, and by the 1983 general election over 400 candidates had been assessed in this way.[18] When a constituency association is looking for a candidate, it is expected to consult the Vice-Chairman, who usually recommends some names from the list, but inclusion on the list is not essential to selection and local associations can consider other potential candidates also.

In the Labour Party, the selection process cannot begin without permission from the NEC, which keeps two lists of approved candidates: list A is of union-sponsored candidates (over 130 in 1979), list B contains all other potential candidates. Both lists go automatically to a constituency party seeking a candidate. Sponsorship of candidates by a trade union or cooperative society means that the sponsoring body will pay up to 80 per cent of the candidate's election expenses as well as, in many cases, contributing to party funds.

Whereas Conservative Associations normally select from roughly 100 candidates, Constituency Labour Parties usually choose from fewer than twenty. Although there probably are more people interested in becoming Conservative than Labour candidates, the numerical disparity also arises out of a difference in procedure. In the Conservative Party, would-be candidates apply personally for consideration, either directly or via Central Office; in the Labour Party, they have to be nominated to the Constituency Party, on the invitation of its Executive Committee, by affiliated organisations (trade union branches, socialist and women's societies, local cooperative societies, Young Socialist branches and local parties); thus affiliated institutions carry out an initial vetting process.

The NEC can veto candidates if there is any irregularity in the selection procedure as well as on grounds of personal or political unacceptability. Similarly, Central Office can withhold approval from the choice of a Conservative Association. In practice, since 1945 this power has been rarely exercised in either party. Up to 1974, central assent was withheld on only two occasions in the Conservative Party and only slightly more often in the Labour Party; in 1974, however, it does seem that the Conservative Vice-Chairman prevented the adoption of right-wing Powellite candidates in three constituencies, although none of these had appeared on the party's approved list.[19] In 1983, before the Bermondsey by-election, the NEC refused to endorse the candidature of Peter Tatchell (because it thought his views too extreme), but were forced to give way by a local party determined to adopt him.

Local parties, therefore, have formidable powers in the selection process. However, not all local party members are involved. Small subcommittees of the Executive Council (Conservative) and General Management Committee (Labour) draw up short lists from the total candidature. Shortlisted candidates then appear before a final selection conference which is usually the Executive Council in local Conservative Associations and, in

Constituency Labour Parties, the General Management Committee. Their decisions are normally final, though Conservative candidates have to gain the formal approval of a general meeting of the local party membership; this assent is virtually a formality and refusals are very few indeed.[20] In both parties readoption struggles were rare in the thirty years after 1945 and there were only twenty-three in the Conservative Party and a mere twelve in the Labour Party in this period.

The procedure for selecting candidates became an increasingly controversial issue during the 1970s, especially in the Labour Party. In 1975, Reg Prentice, the Labour MP for Newham North-East, was asked to retire by the General Management Committee of his Constituency Labour Party. A number of other Labour MPs at this time also experienced difficulties with their constituency parties. The main issue raised by these cases is the 'representativeness' of the 'activists' who were so fiercely holding their MPs to account. It became very apparent that Labour Party procedures were vulnerable to manipulation by determined extremists, owing to the rapid decline in local membership. Hard work, organisational skill and a knowledge of the rules could enable a determined group to capture a local party; such a group could be on the right of the party as well as on the left. In 1977 two Oxford students, by even more skilful manipulation of the law and the party rule-book, won back control of the North-East Newham Labour Party from the left-wingers who had ousted Prentice. Opponents of this type of 'politicking' do not question the right of a local party to withdraw its support from a sitting Member of Parliament, but consider that the decision should be made by the whole membership of the local party. When the local association refused to readopt Nigel Nicolson, Conservative MP for Bournemouth East, in 1959, the decision was taken on a vote of nearly 7,500 members.[21]

In the 1979–1983 parliament readoption became more uncertain for MPs of both parties. The changes in constituency boundaries introduced on the eve of the 1983 general election made matters difficult for a number of MPs in both parties. But Labour MPs faced even graver problems because of the introduction of a new constitutional requirement of mandatory reselection in 1981. This meant that all sitting Labour MPs had to undergo a reselection meeting with their local constituency parties no later than three years after the previous general election, although all had an automatic right to be shortlisted. Eight Labour MPs were refused reselection before the 1983 general election and about a dozen more who would probably have faced reselection difficulties either defected to the SDP or retired. Twelve Labour MPs and eight Conservative MPs failed to be selected for any of the new seats created by the most radical boundary revision for over sixty years.[22] At the 1984 Labour Party Conference, a proposal to introduce a system of one member one vote at reselection meetings was defeated and could not be revived for a further three years. Meanwhile, local CLPs were preparing to hold another round of reselection meetings and once again a number of Labour MPs were widely reported as being under threat of deselection.

Party finances

Both parties are heavily dependent on outside sources for their income. Table 3.2 sets out the main business and trade union contributors to the parties' funds in 1983. The significance of this institutional support to the two major parties becomes clear when their annual incomes are compared with the incomes of the Liberal Party and the SDP (see Table 3.3) Nonetheless, both the SDP and, to a lesser extent, the Liberal Party raised considerable sums in 1983 from small and large contributors. In real terms, Alliance central spending in the 1983 general election was six times greater than Liberal central spending in the 1979 election.

The Conservative Party is wealthier than the Labour Party. During the early 1970s, its income was consistently twice as much as Labour's. Yet by the second half of the decade the income of both parties was insecure, open to criticism for its major sources and perhaps also too small for their purposes. The Conservatives' income was insecure because it depended on companies which decide their donations on a year-to-year basis. Between 1980–83, the value of company contributions to the Conservatives, including payments to local parties, was barely two-thirds the value of trade unions' contributions to Labour. Conservative Party income is also insecure because party membership is declining and, as a result, local payments to party headquarters are falling.

Table 3.2 *Leading business and trade union contributors to the funds of the two major parties, 1983 (five largest in pounds)*

The Conservative Party		The Labour Party	
		*Total Political Spending**	*Payments to Labour Head office*
British and Commonwealth Shipping	94,050	Transport Workers (TGWU)	1,449,163	1,120,752
		Municipal and Boilermakers Union (GMBTU)	1,164,426	669,305
Allied-Lyons	80,000			
Hanson Trust	80,000	Engineers (AUEW)	940,001	721,020
Taylor-Woodrow	79,035	Public Employees (NUPE)	761,174	520,048
Guardian Royal Exchange	76,000	Miners (NUM)	n.a.	352,650

* excludes administrative expenditure and includes grants to Labour Head office, local Labour parties, MPs, etc.
Source: *The Times*, 4 January 1985

Table 3.3 *Central Party incomes, 1980–1983 (millions of pounds)*

	1980	*1981*	*1982*	*1983*
Conservative	3·2	4·1	4·8	9·8
Labour	2·8*	3·7	3·9	6·1
Liberal	0·2*	0·2	0·3	0·8
SDP		0·9	1·5	1·6

* includes state grant to parliamentary opposition parties
Source: *The Times*, 4 January 1985

In 1983–4 Conservative constituency associations paid £850,000 into Central Office funds, 25 per cent less in real terms than in 1979.[23] In 1983, the unions provided £5·1 million of Labour's central income of £6·1 million. As Table 3.3 demonstrates, the Labour Party does not receive the whole of the political levy raised by unions from their members: unions tend to affiliate to the party at less than the total sums produced by the political levy.[24] They then use the remaining money to sponsor MPs and to fight general election campaigns. (See Table 5.4 for union-sponsored candidates in 1983)

This dependence on firms and unions for revenue has been criticised for two main reasons. First, firms' and unions' donations to the parties seldom represent the expressed wishes of their shareholders or members. Not until the 1967 Companies Act were firms required to disclose their political contributions; even now, undisclosed gifts may be channelled to the Conservative Party through 'front' organisations like British United Industrialists which donated over half a million pounds to the party in 1974. In practice, however, it is doubtful whether either type of donation (disclosed or undisclosed) can be effectively challenged. In paying their dues, union members contribute automatically to the political levy unless they specifically ask not to (contract out). In 1982, sixty-three trade unions had political funds and forty-seven of them were affiliated to the Labour Party. The four largest unions in 1983 (TGWU, AUEW, GMWU and NUPE) provided the party with nearly half its funds as well as making over 50 per cent of the unions' contribution to Labour's general election funds. The proportion of trade unionists contracting out of the political levy varies from union to union: a majority of members of the white collar and steel unions contract out but very few do so in the big general and industrial unions. Overall, about 20 per cent contract out. However, survey evidence suggests that if asked almost 50 per cent of unionists would vote against their union continuing to possess a political fund.

The second cause for concern was that the financial dependence of the parties increased the likelihood of their being unduly influenced in their policies by their private 'paymasters'. The political independence of parties which could finance such a small proportion of their activities from the subscriptions and fund-raising efforts of their members seemed to be threatened. The decline in party membership in the 1960s and 1970s could only make things worse. The most recent investigation (Houghton Committee, 1976) estimated Conservative membership at just under 1·5 million; it was over 2·75 million in 1953.[25] Labour individual membership, which stood at about 1 million in 1953, had declined to little more than 250,000 in 1978. 5·9 million in that year were affiliated to the party through the trade unions.

The Trade Union Act (1984) provided that union members should vote at least once every ten years on whether the union should continue to contribute money towards political activities. Within fifteen months of the Act every union with a political fund which had not balloted its members on it within the previous ten years would have to hold a ballot on the continuation of the fund. Where a majority was against a political fund, unions would have to transfer these assets to a non-political fund within six months. But the Act does not require trade unionists to 'contract in' rather than 'contract out' of the political levy. After discussions with the government, the TUC agreed to issue its own code of practice spelling out the rights of trade unionists not to pay the political levy as part of their subscriptions.

The impact of the Act upon Labour Party finances may be less severe than some critics expected. If, for example, union officials who support political funds organise effectively and pick an advantageous moment to hold their ballots, their members could well vote in favour of continuing the political funds. Moreover, assuming some unions vote against their continuance, those that do vote in favour could offset such a loss to the Labour Party by raising their subscriptions. When such a large union as the TGWU increased its subscription from 13 pence to 39 pence in 1984, the increase enabled it to collect an additional £1·5 million per annum. Moreover, companies, whose gifts to the Conservative Party have declined over the last decade, may become more reluctant to make their contributions if some unions end their Labour Party levies.

Finally, party income has become too small to support an agent in each constituency as well as central staff of the size and quality which many contend a democracy requires. The Conservative Party had 320 agents and Labour sixty-two in 1983. In 1976 the Houghton Committee on Financial Aid to Political Parties recommended state grants to political parties. Some financial aid to opposition parties was in fact begun in 1975. The Conservatives received £150,000, the Liberals, £33,250, the SNP, £9,700 and three smaller parties a total of £10,620. Houghton proposed much larger sums, with allocations at the national level being made according to the electoral support of each party and local parties receiving small contributions towards the expenses of candidates in local government and parliamentary elections. In 1976 the total cost of state aid to the parties under the Houghton proposals would have been £2·25 million, although the Committee was anxious that the government grants should not exceed 20 per cent of the parties' total incomes.[26] These recommendations were very controversial (four of the committee dissented from the report) and there was little sign of their adoption by 1979. Opponents argued that state aid for voluntary organisations would be a break with a valuable tradition, that it would compel taxpayers to support organisations with whose principles they did not agree and that the parties' membership fees were relatively low and should be raised.

This chapter had described the political ideas, programmes and organisation of the two major parties. The next chapter focuses on the minor parties, whose upsurge has been such an important feature of British politics in the 1970s and 1980s.

4 The Minor Parties

In the 1983 general election, minor parties in Great Britain (excluding Ulster) polled over 8 million votes. Although their parliamentary reward was small – a mere twenty-seven seats, *electorally* they were a force to be reckoned with. No fewer than forty-four MPs from small parties were returned in this election when we take into account Northern Ireland, whose party system is a law unto itself, but whose MPs sit in the Westminster parliament. This result confirmed a trend observable since the early 1970s – the displacement of a broadly two-party system by a more various scene, at least in the constituencies. Whilst most of the smaller parties and groupings do not expect to form a government – and the one that did so aspire (the Alliance) had its hopes savagely dashed – the upsurge of electoral support for them upset the major parties. Twenty years previously, in the 1964 general election, votes for the Scottish and Welsh nationalist parties numbered tens rather than hundreds of thousands, Ulster Unionists were political associates of the Conservatives and there was no National Front. More significantly, there was no SDP and no Alliance. By contrast, in 1983, the nationalist parties counted their support – now lower than in the mid-1970s – still in hundreds of thousands; the Ulster Unionists had severed themselves from the Conservative Party; and a number of political groupings on the extreme right had come into existence. But it was the SDP-Liberal Alliance which really transformed the electoral picture, polling 7·75 million and taking 26 per cent of the poll. Its arrival as a serious political force added to – in the geographical sense, completed – the fragmentation and regionalisation of British electoral politics.

Minor parties therefore merit serious consideration in any textbook account of contemporary British politics. What this chapter is concerned to do, is to ask about the smaller political parties the kind of questions concerning leadership, organisation, ideology, policy, membership and support which were posed about the two major parties. It is also important to try to account for their increasing significance at this stage in the nation's history. We begin with the Liberal Party.

The Liberal Party

The Liberal Party differs from other smaller parties in the sense that it was once a major party and would like to be one again. There are two main difficulties in the way of this goal – first, the workings of the British electoral system with its remorseless squeeze upon third parties; second, the problem of political credibility. After the February 1974 general election a ray of hope shone. To retain power himself, the Conservative Prime Minister Edward Heath, whose majority had been swept away, sought a deal with the Liberals. The Liberals, whose last experience of peace-time power had been in 1932, dithered, and were lost. They had not worked out a strategy to deal with such a situation. The moment passed. Harold Wilson formed a minority Labour Government which achieved an overall parliamentary majority seven months later in the second election of that year. The episode contained a lesson for Liberals: in order to broaden their appeal to voters, they might have to be ready to sacrifice their political independence, and make agreements with other parties. Alliance might provide the best stepping-stone from being a party of protest to becoming one of government.

Three years later, when opportunity arose again for the exercise of national influence, the Liberal Party was better prepared. On 19 March 1977 the Conservative and Scottish National parties both tabled motions of no confidence in the Labour Government. Since November 1976 the Labour Government had lacked an overall majority in the House of Commons and the only way of securing a reliable majority, short of risking a general election which it wished to avoid, was to make an arrangement with one or more of the minor parties. By the end of the following week, the Prime Minister had concluded an agreement with the Liberal Party which, renewed in the summer of 1977, was to last for eighteen months.[1] In return for their voting support in the House of Commons, Liberals were given the opportunity to get some of their policies adopted by the Government. The pact was made public, would last for a fixed period (initially the end of the parliamentary session on October 1977) and involved the establishment of a joint (Labour-Liberal) consultative committee chaired by the Leader of the House, Michael Foot, to examine government and Liberal legislative proposals before they went before parliament. There were also to be regular meetings between the Chancellor of the Exchequer, Denis Healey, and the Liberal spokesman, John Pardoe, to discuss economic affairs. Specific proposals put by the Liberals to the government included legislation for direct elections to the European Parliament (with a free vote on the question of proportional representation) and separate Bills for the devolution of power to Scottish and Welsh Assemblies, with amendments to take account of Liberal ideas. The government agreed, and, with the aid of Liberal votes, defeated the motion of no confidence on 24 March by 322–298. The main national effect of the Lib-Lab Pact was to enable the Labour Government to stay in office for a further two years. But it had deep significance for the Liberal Party also. During the following months and years, it consolidated its commitment to the strategy begun with the pact. Its hope was to take advantage of a 'hung' parliament situation (in which neither major party has a majority) to negotiate for its own policies, especially proportional representation, as its 'price' for sustaining either in government. What sort of party is this small party which gained in 1977–8 its best chance to exercise direct political influence since its minor role in the war-time coalition of Winston Churchill a generation previously?

The Liberal Party contains a wider range of political views than any other party: it includes traditional Liberalism going back to the 1930s and 'moderate' Liberalism which is well represented in the parliamentary party, as well as the Young Liberals whose politics is to the left of most of the Labour Party. Traditional Liberalism is distinguished from the other two varieties by its social conservatism: older Liberals tend to favour the *status quo*; by contrast, other strands in Liberalism are for reform. David Steel, who became Liberal leader in 1976, introduced legislation to reform the abortion law in 1967 and Young Liberals have campaigned strongly for equal rights for homosexuals. On economic policy, traditional Liberalism has a *laissez-faire* emphasis, moderate Liberals favour incomes policies and government intervention in the economy while Young Liberals in their 1979 manifesto opposed incomes policies because they held down the wages of the lower-paid. The older generation of Liberals recall the internationalism of an earlier period, but Young Liberals have taken a more uncompromising attitude to international politics: in the 1960s, they called for British withdrawal from NATO, non-alignment in the Cold War and massive reductions in armaments. In particular, they have taken a particularly determined stand against racialism: they pressed David Steel in 1976 to declare his support for the liberation movements in Southern Africa and three years later, strongly opposed the 1971 Immigration Act for bringing a 'specifically racial tone' to the British immigration laws.

One issue which apparently unites the party is concern for the individual. But, in practice, Liberals often have rather different images of the 'individual'. For 'moderate' and traditional Liberals, he is the 'little man' who feels threatened by the 'big battalions' – the large firms, big retail stores and the unions. For such Liberals, the 'individual' is the person whose right to join a union needs to be protected against employers and whose right *not* to join against the unions. Liberal Party manifestoes habitually criticise the two major parties for their close links with business and the trade unions. But Young Liberals have been less hostile to the unions. Differences of strategy within the party are also acute. The Liberal leadership believes in parliamentary methods of achieving the radical changes it seeks. When it advocates an end to the two-party system it is asking for more Liberals to be elected to parliament: its short-term goal is sufficient Liberal MPs to hold the balance between the major parties. Electoral reform by the introduction of proportional representation is advocated not only as intrinsically fairer but also as the best way to attain this goal.

The style of the Young Liberals, however, is populist in emphasis, stressing participatory rather than parliamentary democracy. They have even been prepared to advocate extra-constitutional methods: their 1979 manifesto, *Fighting for To-*

morrow, recommended direct action if other ways of achieving desired changes fail. 'Although it need not be illegal we are prepared to break the law if necessary.'

In the 1960s, modelling themselves on the US campaigners for civil rights, they pioneered 'community politics'. Community politics involves encouraging people to fight for improvements in their local communities and for this reason has often been termed 'paving slab' politics. It seeks to involve people actively in a struggle for greater control over their own lives – at the workplace, in local government, in local schools, hospitals and so on. Its stress is upon the politics of *campaigning* which is almost erected into an end in itself. It depends upon constant leaflet distribution and the willingness of Liberal candidates and campaigners to concern themselves with any local issue no matter how small. In the late 1970s the advocates of 'community politics' developed another strong base within the party in the Association of Liberal Councillors (ALC). Its organising secretary, Tony Greaves, is a Lancashire councillor and a former chairman of the Young Liberals. The political weight of the ALC stems partly from its resources: as well as its own headquarters at Hebden Bridge in West Yorkshire, the ALC has an annual budget of £80,000, six full-time staff, an information bank, a sizeable library, three regular publications, and a computer programmed to serve its members (1983). But it also derives from the party's considerable success as a campaigning force in local elections: in the autumn of 1983, there were 2,000 Liberal councillors, the party controlled six councils and held the balance of power in twenty others. During the early 1980s, tension between the leadership, on the one hand, and the YLs and ALC, on the other, continued over both policy and strategy. On policy, Britain's nuclear deterrent was a leading source of controversy, with unilateralist Young Liberals facing a multilateralist leadership. On strategy, the anxieties of grass-roots Liberals were expressed during the 1983 election campaign by the ALC which criticised the Alliance manifesto for dropping or diluting certain Liberal policies. After the election, the YLs tried at the 1983 Conference to remove the leader's veto on the manifesto; this was defeated, but by a smaller margin (broadly a 2:1 majority) than the leadership would have liked. A move to provide the party with a deputy leader, who would serve as a check upon the leader, was not accepted either. But the tension between a strategy of national alliance-building from the top by media-orientated Westminster politicians and one of building up strength from the bottom by door-stepping activists remains.

Like the two main parties, the Liberal Party consists of an organisation in the country and a central bureaucracy as well as a group of MPs at Westminster. At the grass-roots level, the party is composed of constituency associations which are themselves grouped in a broadly federal structure into twelve English regions, Ulster, Wales and Scotland. Liberals can also join the party's 'recognised bodies', two of the most important of which have been noticed already: the National League of Young Liberals and the Association of Liberal Councillors. Others include the Women's Liberal Federation, the Union of Liberal Students and the Liberal Candidates' Association. All sides of the party meet at the Annual Assembly (conference), which includes representatives from the constituency associations and 'recognised bodies' together with agents and organisers from the party headquarters (its civil service) and MPs and parliamentary candidates. The Assembly debates policy and elects both the Liberal Council and the President and officers of the party organisation in England and Wales. The Council pronounces on current political issues between assemblies and is responsible for fund-raising, the adoption of candidates and the maintenance of the party headquarters. The headquarters provides administrative services for the party and carries out propaganda, publicity and research.

As in the major parties, much work is done by small committees. The main ones are the Finance and Administration Board; the National Executive Committee; and the Standing Committee. The Finance and Administration Board is the key committee at headquarters. It contains the Secretary-General (i.e. the head of the whole party organisation) whom it appoints as well as the Treasurer. The Finance and Administration Committee is elected by and in a broad sense responsible to the National Executive (NEC). The NEC is appointed by the Council – a large body which meets only quarterly – to be responsible for the day-to-day affairs of the party. The majority of the Standing Committee, whose meetings are chaired by an MP (Clement Freud in 1983), are elected by the Council, adopted candidates and MPs. The Standing Committee serves to bring together the parliamentary and non-parliamentary sides of the party. It looks after long-term policy development, expresses opinion on urgent political issues and, in general, coordinates party affairs. On matters of campaigning and strategy, its responsibilities overlap with those of the NEC. A number of organisational changes followed the 1983 election. Under its Secretary-General (John Spiller), the Liberals began a major exercise of regional administrative devolution within the party: eight central headquarters staff were sacked as part of a plan to devote 30 per cent of the Party's £400,000 annual budget to the funding of new staff appointments in the regions: this reduced the central staff to twenty-eight. At the same time, following the open differences of opinion between various sections of the party during and after the election, a working party consisting of four ALC representatives, three MPs and the chairman of the Liberal Parliamentary Association was established to assist the coordination of strategy.

The Liberal Party has adopted a fully democratic method in the election of its leader. As a result of a change introduced in 1976, the leader of the party is elected by the party membership by secret ballot in each constituency. Electoral votes are allocated to each constituency according to the length of its affiliation to the party and the number of votes its candidate received at the previous general election. When the party members have voted, the votes allocated to each constituency are divided between the leadership candidates in proportion to the membership votes each has gained. The result of the first leadership election conducted by the new method in July 1976 was: David Steel, 12,541 electoral votes; John Pardoe, 7,032 electoral votes.

The Liberals did well in the parliamentary elections of 1974 and 1979 without, however, achieving the political breakthrough they hoped for. (Table 4.1). The party's best result was in February 1974 when it won 14 seats, gained over 6 million votes – half as many as each of the major parties – and got just under one-fifth of the total vote. But its very considerable support at the polls was not translated into parliamentary seats. Under the

Table 4.1 *The Liberal Party: votes, parliamentary seats, candidates and share of the total vote, 1945–79*

Election	Votes	Seats	Candidates	Percentage of total vote
1945	2,248,226	12	306	9·0
1950	2,621,548	9	475	9·1
1951	730,556	6	109	2·5
1955	722,405	6	110	2·7
1959	1,638,571	6	216	5·9
1964	3,092,878	9	365	11·2
1966	2,327,533	12	311	8·5
1970	2,117,035	6	332	7·5
1974 Feb.	6,063,470	14	517	19·3
1974 Oct.	5,346,754	13	619	18·3
1979	4,313,931	11	575	13·8

Sources: D. Butler and A. Sloman, *British Political Facts 1900–1975*, Macmillan, pp. 184–6; *The Guardian*, 5 May 1979

simple majority system, it took over ten times as many votes to elect a Liberal MP than to elect a Conservative or Labour MP. With a system of proportional representation, the Liberals would have won over 120 seats in October 1974; as it was, their 5·25 million votes gained them only thirteen seats. Nonetheless, a Liberal revival did take place in the 1960s and 1970s. Even in 1979, when its vote fell sharply from the peak of 1974, the party had still doubled its popular support and parliamentary representation over the previous two decades. This resurgence of the party continued in the general election of 1983 which the Liberals fought in concert with the SDP as 'the Alliance'. The new political grouping got an aggregate vote of 7,775,040, approximately 1·75 million votes more than the best previous achievement of the Liberals when fighting alone (February 1974). Although they were still a long way from the *parliamentary* breakthrough they sought, the Liberals had increased their representation in the House of Commons to seventeen – their highest since the war.

There have been several persistent strands in Liberal policies. They have consistently advocated reform of the political system, taking proportional representation and the devolution of power to Scotland, Wales and the English regions as their main goals. They were quick to propose entry to the Common Market and, after British membership of the EEC was gained, they strongly supported direct elections to the European parliament. In the 1970s, their traditional concern for the individual resulted in the advocacy of a Bill of Rights to guarantee civil liberties and to protect the citizen against all kinds of discrimination. In 1984, the Liberal leader David Steel became the main sponsor of a Freedom of Information Bill intended to combat a secretive system of government which was widely regarded as eroding the rights of the individual. Liberals believe in a statutory incomes policy and are firmly committed to industrial co-partnership involving profit-sharing and worker participation on works councils based on election by all employees and not just by the trade unions. They want taxes on wealth, more help for small businesses and a radical reform of the tax system by the introduction of credit income tax.

Liberals pride themselves on being the party with bright ideas. Certainly, many of their ideas have subsequently been introduced by governments, but it is unlikely that the enactment of such policies as entry to the EEC or the expansion of higher education in the 1960s owed anything to Liberal pressure. Most governments since the war have had comfortable majorities and have not had to listen to the Liberals. And even the adoption of policies of devolution by the major parties was a response to nationalist pressure not to Liberal advocacy. Liberals would claim, however, that their 1977–78 agreement with Labour brought a change. They say that the pact brought benefits both to the nation and to their party. Its primary achievement was to provide a period of stable government vital to the fight against inflation and to the revival of business confidence. Because of it, the divisive policies of Labour's left-wing extremists were held in check; nationalisation, for instance. Liberals pushed the government into important concessions on its devolution proposals and successfully pressed for the introduction of profit-sharing schemes. They also won some smaller changes on policies relating to small businesses, direct elections to the European Parliament, taxation and farming. Critics contend that the pact primarily benefitted the Labour Party which got an extended tenure of office very cheaply. The main effect of the agreement was to prevent a general election being held in 1977, which almost certainly the Conservatives would have won. The Liberals enabled the Labour Government to continue with its own economic policies but whether these were better for the country than the Conservative alternative is a matter of judgement. Concessions won on devolution were significant but others were very minor and lacked popular appeal. Changes that the Liberals most wanted – proportional representation for the Scottish and Welsh Assemblies and for the European parliament – were not achieved. During 1977, opposition to the pact increased from Liberals who feared its electoral consequences for the party, and on 25 May 1978, David Steel formally terminated it.

Nonetheless, as has been seen, the Liberal strategy of alliance-building did not stop there. A year later, it received a further stimulus from the 1979 election campaign. Questioned about their voting behaviour, 29 per cent of Conservative voters and 28 per cent of Labour voters said they would have voted for the Liberals if Liberal prospects of success had been greater. Had they voted Liberal, the party would have received 34 per cent of the three-party vote. Contacts with Labour politicians increased – a policy begun by David Steel in 1976 with an open letter to Shirley Williams. Two years later, the quest for a realignment of the left reached a further stage with the formation of the SDP.

The Social Democratic Party

A press conference held in the Connaught Rooms, London, on 26 March 1981 signalled the birth of the new party.[2] It consisted initially of fifteen former Labour MPs (thirteen of whom were current Members of Parliament) and one former Conservative MP. Special public attention focussed upon the four ex-Labour Cabinet Ministers who had taken the initiative in founding the party: Roy Jenkins, Shirley Williams, David Owen and William Rodgers. It was the last-named three politicians – the so-called 'gang of three' – whose Limehouse Declaration earlier in the year presaged the formation of the SDP by setting up the Council for

Social Democracy. This statement – so termed because it was issued from David Owen's home in Limehouse – laid down the operating principles of the new political grouping (whose founders at that stage were still members of the Labour Party). Internationally, the 'gang of three' supported the EEC, NATO, and multilateral efforts to secure arms control and relieve Third World poverty. Domestically, they favoured a mixed economy with healthy public and private sectors and fewer 'frontier changes' between the two; more decentralisation of decision-making in industry and government together with an effective system of workplace democracy; and, finally, a more positive effort to tackle the problem of mass unemployment. The party which, having been joined by Roy Jenkins, they went on to found, was a radical centrist grouping. Rejecting the ideological 'extremism' and subjection to the big economic interest groups (business and unions) of the two major parties, the Social Democratic Party (SDP) sought a political realignment of the forces of moderate reform opposed to both.

The origins of the SDP have to be looked for primarily in the disillusionment of certain right-wing Labour politicians with trends within their own party. In the Limehouse Declaration, the 'gang of three' rejected 'the drift towards extremism' in the Labour Party, condemning its steady movement 'away from its roots in the people of this country and its commitment to parliamentary government'. Their immediate cause for concern was the failure of the Labour Party constitutional conference in December 1980 to adopt the principle of 'one man, one vote' in the selection of the leader by members of the party. They strongly opposed its adoption of a mode of selection which gave such a prominent role to the trade unions. This change when taken together with other tendencies in the party suggested its increasing domination by a rigid and insular far left. They particularly deplored the growing support within the party for a 'siege economy' based on import controls; for major extensions of public ownership, trade union powers and State planning apparatus; unilateralism; and for withdrawal from the EEC. Both unilateralism and withdrawal from the Common Market had been endorsed by the 1980 Party Conference and the three had signalled their opposition at the time whilst avowing their commitment to democratic socialism. They had no faith in the ability of its recently-elected leader, Michael Foot, to arrest the growing influence within the party of policies and attitudes which they saw as not only wrong in principle but also as likely to prove electorally disastrous. But the origins of the new party have also to be sought in the political convictions of Roy Jenkins, a former Labour Home Secretary and Chancellor of the Exchequer in the 1960s, and in the political calculations of the Liberal leader, David Steel. Jenkins was a front-rank political figure of proven liberal views, a convinced 'European', whose commitment to the EEC culminated in a spell as President of the European Commission. On his return from Brussels in 1979, he raised the possibility of a new centre political grouping in the Dimbleby Lecture before a large television audience. For his part, Steel had continued the search for a re-grouping of the left begun by the previous Liberal leader, Jo Grimond, in the 1960s, most notably in his practice of cross-party collaboration in the EEC Referendum campaign (1975) and in the Lib-Lab Pact (1977) and by his constant efforts to persuade disaffected Labour politicians to join such an enterprise. Why did he not simply seek to persuade them to join the Liberal Party rather than to form a new one? It was in effect his calculation that two parties in alliance stood a better chance of making a breakthrough in the political centre than one party alone.

The SDP made considerable progress in its first year. Under its initially 'collective' leadership, it recruited a membership of 70,000, gained funds of £650,000 and, most significant of all, won several important by-election victories. Roy Jenkins began the process by making considerable inroads into the sizeable Labour majority at Warrington in July 1981 and this achievement was followed by victories for Shirley Williams at Crosby (November 1981) and for Jenkins himself at Glasgow Hillhead (March 1982). In keeping with its beliefs, the SDP speedily formed an alliance with the Liberals (June 1981) which resulted in a joint statement of principles entitled *A Fresh Start for Britain*. By December 1981, the Alliance was at the top (46 per cent) in the opinion polls and was talking of 'holding the balance' in the next parliament, even of forming a government. Then came the Falklands War. Public support for the Alliance fell, stabilizing at around

20–25 per cent in the early months of 1983, the eve of the general election.

By this time the SDP had acquired both a constitution and a single leader. The main decisions on the procedure for electing the leader of the party were taken at a Constitutional Convention held at Kennington in February 1982. This provided for the election of a leader of the Parliamentary Committee (the SDP leader) and a President, both by a postal ballot of the membership. Under this system, Roy Jenkins became the party's first leader, defeating David Owen by 26,300 votes to 20,900, and Shirley Williams, whose rivals were William Rodgers and Stephen Haseler, its first President. By later in the year, a policy-making procedure had also been developed. At the grass-roots level, constituencies were grouped into Areas, each with a minimum membership of 200–300. The most important tasks of the Area party groups are candidate selection and participation in policy-making by the election of representatives to the Council for Social Democracy on a 'one member, one vote' basis. At the top, the key groups are the Policy Committee and the Council for Social Democracy. The Policy Committee, whose membership is equally divided between MPs and others, decides the membership and terms of reference of twenty-five policy groups. In the first instance, policy proposals are published as Green Papers; then, after consideration of comments by Area groups and outside interests, they are reformulated as White Papers. The Council for Social Democracy consists of 400 members and meets three to four times per year with the President as chairperson. Its role in policy-making interlocks with the Policy Committee. As the peak SDP institution, in formal terms, it has the final say on policy, but it does not itself develop policy; it does not amend the proposals emanating from the Policy Committee, merely – if unsatisfied – referring them back to that Committee for further work.

The SDP fought the 1983 general election in close association with the Liberal Party as 'the Alliance'. The joint SDP-Liberal manifesto entitled *Working Together for Britain* further developed the proposals of the first joint statement of June 1981. The Alliance stood for an end to the old two-party politics of class war and confrontation. It proposed a 'fairer' electoral system, a moderate stimulus to the economy and an 'internationalist' foreign policy. The close links between constitutional reform and an improvement of Britain's economic performance were stressed: a more just electoral system would provide greater political stability by strengthening the 'moderate' centre against the 'extremes'. It would thereby terminate the adversarial politics with its frequent reversals of policy on, for example, incomes policy, the trade unions, and the management of the economy. The Alliance ran candidates in 633 constituencies. However, after an early decision (December 1981) to fight roughly the same number of seats each, the two parties became locked in a well-publicised dispute about the precise share-out. The Liberals – a party with a strong grass-roots organisation, which had come second in eighty-one seats in 1979 – were reluctant to stand down in constituencies they regarded as winnable. They got the best of the bargain in the compromise eventually reached (January 1982), retaining their fifty most promising seats; the SDP received two-thirds of the 100 next best constituencies. As it happened, this allocation was to have a decisive bearing on the relative fortunes of the Alliance partners. In order to stand any chance of being elected, candidates allocated the less attractive seats would need to achieve an improbable 35 per cent share of the poll. As has been seen, the Alliance polled well in the 1983 general election. Its total vote was 7·75 million, only 700,000 short of the Labour Party's. Its share of the total vote was 26 per cent compared with Labour's 28·3 per cent and represented nearly a doubling of the Liberal share of the vote in 1979 (13·8 per cent). But only twenty-three of its candidates were elected – in dramatic contrast with Labour's 209, even if this figure did more than double the number of Liberal MPs after 1979 (eleven). As expected, more Liberal (seventeen) than SDP (six) candidates were returned, a result which constituted in effect five more Liberals and twenty-four fewer SDP MPs than in the previous parliament. Under a system of proportional representation, the Alliance would have obtained 150 seats or more. As it was, not only had it not cracked the mould of British politics, one of its two components, the SDP, was reduced to one-fifth of its former size. There were, of course, some bright spots in a generally bleak picture. Its share of the total vote was higher than any achieved by the Liberals alone since 1923: the politics of party alliance was obviously popular with the electorate. It had demonstrated its ability to draw support from all social groups. Moreover, it had achieved second place in 312 constituencies – a platform here for future progress.

The election was followed by the immediate resignation of Roy Jenkins, ostensibly to avoid a damaging leadership contest with David Owen. Jenkins had fought an honourable campaign and had done well to hold his Glasgow Hillhead constituency, but Owen had done better. His political star was in the ascendant; he was one of the few non-Conservative politicians to have enhanced his reputation during the Falklands War and he had fought a successful election campaign both in his own constituency of Plymouth Devonport and on the national stage. But, after succeeding uncontested to the leadership, he faced immediate difficulties within the party. Membership declined to just over 50,000 by September 1984, a drop of 14,000 from the figure two years previously. After an expensive campaign, the party faced financial difficulties and had to make drastic cuts in its central staff. This went down from fifty-five to twenty-three immediately after the election and had stabilised at thirty by the autumn of 1984. The most serious problem was the SDP's relationship with the Liberals. Owen himself was anxious to maintain the party's separate identity, taking a 'harder' line on this issue than Jenkins had done. David Steel, on the other hand, was known to favour closer relations. The Liberal-SDP Pact on candidate selection (January 1984) required a joint committee of the parties at national level to approve proposals emanating from the local parties, an arrangement which would probably assist Owen in severely restricting the number of constituencies with joint selection. Another well-publicised difference in 1983–4 was over defence policy, with the Liberals (notwithstanding the objections of their leader) against the siting of Cruise missiles in Britain and the SDP supportive of Cruise. The only way in which the two parties might come together on this issue was in an agreement on no *further* deployment of Cruise. But the parties did agree on the need for constitutional reforms. Their joint document *Towards a New Constitutional Settlement* (September 1983) recommended proportional representation for all elections; reform of the House of Lords into a part-elected, part-nominated body; substantial devolution of power to Scotland and lesser devolution to Wales and, if the public wanted it, to the English regions; the replacement of rates by a local income tax; a Bill of Rights; and a Freedom of Information Act to create a public right of access to official documents, protect individuals from the misuse of information held on them and safeguard personal privacy.

Meanwhile, a series of policy statements in 1983–4, especially by Dr Owen, helped to define the SDP position on a range of social and economic issues. In so doing, they continued to fuel the debate which had existed since its foundation on whether the SDP was basically a centre-right or centre-left party. In the eyes of its leader, and in the interpretations of most political commentators, the SDP was a left of centre radical alternative to Labour. It favoured a 'social market' economy, emphasising *both* the role of the private sector in wealth creation *and* the role of the State in the management of the economy. Government should stimulate demand by increasing public investment and by industrial credit schemes and should actively promote new technology. On social policy, the SDP supported tax reforms which would help the poorest groups by re-channelling the wealth of middle-income earners and opposed subsidies for private education and private medicine. On trade union reform, the SDP advocated a system of 'contracting in' to the political levy – an individualist position which placed the onus upon individual trade unionists to decide whether or not they wanted to contribute to party funds. But this proposal was balanced by the suggestion that shareholders equally should have the power to ratify the political donations of companies. Trade unions, in the SDP view, should hold ballots of their members before calling strikes.

The prospects for the SDP and for the Alliance at the mid-point between general elections were delicately balanced. On the one hand, despite a somewhat disappointing showing in the elections to the European Parliament (June 1984), the Alliance could be satisfied with its record in the local elections (May 1984) when it won 435 seats (Liberal 375, SDP 60) against the Conservatives 1219 and Labour's 1836 and even more pleased with its performance in by-elections. Although it failed to win any of these constituencies, its share of the poll in the Chesterfield,

Surrey South-West, Stafford and Clwyd by-elections in the first half of 1984 averaged 34–35 per cent. Then, unexpectedly, it won Portsmouth South (June 1984) destroying a Conservative majority of over 12,000 and gaining 37·5 per cent of the poll in the process. The base of its support was consistently higher than any third party had registered in the post-war period and also a great deal higher than the Liberals received on their own in the late 1970s. With the intensity and extent of support for the two major parties in decline and between one-third and two-fifths of electors changing allegiances or moving into or away from abstentions between elections, opportunity beckoned. But the size of the task could not be underestimated. The Alliance needed 37–39 per cent of the national vote to become the largest single party and 30–34 per cent merely to hold the balance. In a situation in which both major parties trimmed their extremist fringes in order to compete in the 'middle ground' of politics, this would be a formidable achievement.

The Scottish National Party
The Scottish National Party was established in 1934 but enjoyed little success in parliamentary elections until the 1970s when tides of popular opinion began to run strongly in its favour. In October 1974, the party polled over three-quarters of a million votes and returned eleven MPs to Westminster. Between 1970 and October

Table 4.2 *The Scottish National Party in general elections, 1959–83*

Election	Votes	Seats	Candidates	Percentage of total vote
1959	21,738		5	0·1
1964	64,044		15	0·2
1966	128,474		20	0·2
1970	306,802	1	65	1·1
1974 Feb.	632,032	7	70	2·0
1974 Oct.	839,617	11	71	2·9
1979	504,259	2	71	1·6
1983	331,975	2	72	1·1

Sources: D. Butler and A. Sloman, *British Political Facts, 1900–1975*, Macmillan, pp. 184–6; *The Guardian*, 5 May 1979; *The Times*, 11 June 1983

1974, in fact, its popular vote nearly trebled and its parliamentary representation increased elevenfold (Table 4.2). Moreover, its share of the Scottish vote rose from a mere 5 per cent to 30·4 per cent in the eight years after 1966. From being a vehicle of romantic cultural nationalism, the SNP became, in the late 1960s and early 1970s, a serious and credible political party.

Events after 1945 totally transformed the character of the Party. In post-war Scotland, unemployment has been persistently higher than the UK average and income per head has been lower. Old heavy industries have continued to decline; inner city areas have decayed; and emigration has remained higher than in most other European countries.[3] All this fuelled resentment at Scotland's lack of control over her economy and industry. The SNP linked this feeling to a sense of national cultural identity and a dislike of remote bureaucratic government. Its battle-cry 'putting Scotland first' drew attention to the mismanagement of Westminster parliaments. Then, in the late 1960s, the discovery of offshore oil suddenly afforded Scotland the prospect of becoming 'one of the richest countries in the world'. The SNP claimed that revenues from oil could be used to re-equip industry, improve education and the social services and reduce the national debt. The slogan 'It's Scotland's oil' lay behind the dramatic rise of the party in the early 1970s.

The ultimate political aim of the SNP is independence for Scotland. In its October 1974 manifesto, *Scotland's Future*, the party demanded a Scottish parliament as a preliminary step to full self-government. It favoured a single-chamber legislature with provision for the holding of referenda.[4] It intends to rescind the Act of Union (1707) and to seek a constitutional position similar to that of Canada, Australia and New Zealand. It maintains that, with a population of 5·75 million and an area of 30,000 square miles, Scotland is larger than many other states which have achieved self-government in the twentieth century: Eire, Norway, Finland and Iceland. In the SNP vision of the future, Wales would also gain independence, and the United Kingdom would become an association of 'free and equal nations' like the Nordic Council of Scandinavia.[5] Scotland would form a common defence policy and a customs union with the rest of the British Isles.

The SNP is a decentralised party which draws its strength from the effectiveness of its local branches. Its democratic ideals are reflected in the constitutional importance of its annual conference and in its practice of collective leadership by two major committees (the National Executive and the National Council). In 1984, its chairman was Gordon Wilson.

In the first six months of 1979, the SNP suffered two severe setbacks. The first blow came on 1 March when the Scottish electorate in a referendum failed to give the proposed Assembly for which the nationalists had campaigned the required 40 per cent support. Nationalists argued that there was a majority, albeit a small one, for the scheme (51·6 per cent of voters, 32·5 per cent of the electorate, were in favour, 48·3 per cent and 30·4 per cent respectively, against it) and that the government should therefore press ahead with devolution for Scotland. But in fact the Labour Cabinet did not consider such a positive step to be justified in the light of the very weak endorsement of its policy. Worse was to follow. At the general election of 1979, the SNP, whose support in Scottish public opinion had declined steadily after reaching a peak of 36 per cent in 1976, lost 300,000 votes and nine of its eleven parliamentary seats. Only two of its MPs, Donald Stewart in the Western Isles and Gordon Wilson in Dundee East, were successful. Its share of the Scottish poll declined by over 13 per cent to 17·3 per cent. The two major parties reasserted themselves, winning nearly three-quarters of Scottish votes and sixty-six (of the seventy-one) Scottish seats. The downward slide of the SNP continued at the 1983 general election. Although its two MPs retained their seats, its total vote fell to just under 332,000 and its share of the Scottish poll to 12 per cent. Forty-eight of its candidates lost their deposits. Electorally, the party had virtually returned to its position in 1970. Its fortunes had declined almost as rapidly as they had arisen. How may this be explained?

There were certain underlying weaknesses in the SNP position even at the height of its success. These weaknesses concern the attitude of Scots to United Kingdom membership; electoral strategy against the other parties; and internal divisions. First, it is doubtful whether a majority of Scots ever really favoured independence from the rest of the United Kingdom. In 1979, they showed themselves divided on devolution and an SNP election campaign which began, undaunted, with the slogan, 'Scotland said Yes, will you let Westminster say No?' fell rather flat. A party so dependent upon a single issue was inevitably hard hit when barely a third of the Scottish electorate endorsed it in a referendum. Second, the SNP has to defend and win seats not only against the two major parties but also the Liberals (after 1981, the Alliance). The sheer number of its opponents raises problems of strategy. In 1974, at its peak, its electoral success concealed a relative weakness in the largest cities, Glasgow, Edinburgh and Aberdeen; its strength in the new towns and with socially mobile, non-unionised and younger voters was offset by the relative failure of its appeal in the larger urban areas and with the unionised, the poorer-off and older voters. Five years later, its share of the vote was still twice as large in rural areas (25 per cent) as it was in Strathclyde (12·8 per cent). When in 1979, the Conservatives took seven of its seats and Labour two, these two parties increased their share of the poll at SNP expense more or less equally – the Conservatives by 6·7 per cent, Labour by 5·2 per cent. Thereafter, the SNP faced a dilemma: should it adopt a more 'moderate' approach on social and economic policy in order to recapture the anti-Tory vote in the north-east which it won in 1974 or should it assume a left-wing stance in order to challenge Labour in the central belt? This was a hard question to resolve. In 1983, moreover, it faced a highly successful campaign by the Alliance which re-asserted traditional Liberal support for home rule, the SNP's own ground, and won eight Scottish seats, a gain of four. Finally, the SNP has had to contend with increasingly severe ideological divisions between its right and left wings. The formation after the 1979 election of a radical left-wing faction, the *79 Group*, committed to bringing about a 'Socialist and Republican' Scotland intensified the turmoil. The struggle within the party came to a head in 1982 with the proscription of the 79 Group and the expulsion of its leading members from the party. These included the SNP's policy vice-chairman, Jim Sillars, and a former vice-chairman, Stephen Maxwell. Another former vice-chairman of the party of left-wing views, Margo MacDonald, resigned. Although those expelled were allowed back in to the party before the 1983 general election, their links with left-wing bodies like the Scottish Socialist Society and Scottish CND remained. The rift was scarcely healed.

Clearly, a number of favouring factors, triggered by oil, came together in the early 1970s to produce a flood tide for the SNP in 1974. The main ones were: electoral 'de-alignment' and the diminishing significance of social class in structuring voters' party allegiances; the policy failures of the two major parties especially with regard to the management of the economy; Britain's entry into the European Economic Community, which seemed to make Scotland more peripheral in UK affairs; and a resurgence of cultural nationalism in Scotland in the 1960s. Despite its failure to acquire a charismatic personality as leader, the SNP had developed an effective organisation which was able to capitalise on these favourable trends. In 1984, it could yet become an effective force again. Notwithstanding reduced membership, which dropped from 80,000 to 20,000 over the previous decade, it still has a core of dedicated activists and a powerful nationalist tradition to draw upon.

Plaid Cymru

Like the SNP, the 'Party of Wales' benefited from a surge of support for nationalist parties in the early 1970s, although its success was much more modest. It gained its first MP in 1966 after a by-election victory but had only increased its representation to three MPs by the end of 1974. Its total vote (about 170,000) held stable between 1970 and 1974, the greatest progress having come in the late 1960s (in 1966, it received just over 60,000 votes, its vote trebling between then and 1970). Plaid Cymru derives the bulk of its support from the rural, Welsh-speaking communities. Nonetheless, the party fought all thirty-six Welsh constituencies in 1974, a considerable advance on the twenty or so candidates it put forward between 1959 and 1966 (Table 4.3).

Plaid Cymru was founded in 1925 and aims at the establishment of a Welsh Parliament as a first step towards the attainment of virtual political independence or 'full national' Commonwealth status. As in Scotland, party propaganda is fuelled by a feeling that Wales gets inferior economic treatment compared with the rest of the UK. The party points to a high incidence of bad

Table 4.3 *Plaid Cymru in general elections, 1959–83*

Election	Votes	Seats	Candidates	Percentage of total vote
1959	77,571	—	20	0·3
1964	69,507	—	23	0·3
1966	61,071	—	20	0·2
1970	175,016	—	36	0·6
1974 Feb.	171,364	2	36	0·6
1974 Oct.	166,321	3	36	0·6
1979	132,544	2	36	0·4
1983	125,309	2	38	0·4

Sources: As for Table 4.2

housing, unemployment and low incomes, and favours steps to diversify an economy over-dependent on mining, steel and agriculture. There is also a feeling of powerlessness in the face of decisions taken by remote companies and government bureaucracies.[6] As in Scotland, the rise of nationalism to political significance in Wales also stems from more general factors, such as the declining prestige of the major political parties and, particularly, the loss of world status by Great Britain, which has raised the possibility of new relationships between the various cultural segments of the UK.

In keeping with its origins, Plaid Cymru aims to preserve and increase the role of the Welsh language in Welsh society. While its spokesmen stress that a sense of Welsh cultural identity is not confined to language, the party nonetheless demands bilingualism 'in all Wales by 2000 A.D.'.[7] The party's stress on the Welsh language is not only a means of expressing anti-materialist values but also provides a link between traditional Welsh culture and contemporary life. The language issue, in fact, is close to the heart of the Welsh nationalist movement; its greater significance is one of the main features distinguishing it from its Scottish counterpart. The hard core of Plaid Cymru's membership is Welsh-speaking and the language issue has particularly important implications in education, broadcasting and public administration. For instance, the party called in 1979 for the immediate establishment of a network of Welsh-medium nursery schools, for the continuation of education of Welsh through the primary and secondary stages for those who wished it and for the introduction of the Welsh language TV channel at least one year earlier than the government-set date of 1982. The Welsh Language Society, founded in 1962 at a Plaid Cymru summer school, campaigns for Welsh to have equality of status with English. In the 1960s and 1970s, it was distinguished from Plaid Cymru by the preparedness of its members to advance their cause by the use of direct action (e.g. the refusal to pay car licence fees). But the percentage of Welsh speakers has been in constant decline since the late nineteenth century (from 60 per cent in 1891 to 19 per cent in 1981). Plaid Cymru's policy, therefore, would reverse the trend of over half a century. Moreover, it is divisive as a political aim and would certainly be resisted by anglicised South Wales, which would fear for employment prospects if bilingualism became the rule.

Wales lacks the natural resources which have given credibility to the Scottish quest for independence. It is also smaller and more dependent upon the rest of the UK. For these reasons, Plaid Cymru, which lacks roots in trade unionism and in local politics, remains more of a cultural pressure and protest group than a political party. In 1979, it used the government's need for its support in the vital 'no confidence' vote to gain an Act to compensate quarrymen and other workers suffering from industrial dust disease. In its 1979 manifesto, the party claimed to have extracted many other concessions of benefit to Wales from Westminster governments, including the establishment of a Welsh Development Agency, a Development Board for Rural Wales and financial help for Welsh language education. Focussing upon short-term objectives, its ten-point plan for economic revival proposed among other things a more energetic policy by the Welsh Development Agency to establish enterprises in areas of need and an expansion of the activities of the Development Corporation to attract more overseas investment to Wales. As one of its MPs, Dafydd Wigley, explained, the party had to fight not only for self-government for Wales but also for the best possible deal for the people of Wales within the status quo.

Like the SNP, the Welsh nationalists experienced setbacks in 1979. Wales rejected the Act which would have set up a Welsh Assembly at Cardiff by the overwhelming margin of 4:1;956,330 – 46·5 per cent of the electorate – voted 'no' in the referendum held on 1 March; a mere 243,048 – 11·8 per cent of electors – voted 'yes'. Like the Scottish nationalists, Plaid Cymru disliked Labour's devolution proposals yet felt obliged to campaign for their acceptance because, imperfect as they were, they were better than nothing and at least were a step on the way towards full self-government. Against this background, the party's rela- tively poor performance in the 1979 general election was hardly surprising. Its total vote shrank by over 30,000 and the party leader, Gwynfor Evans, was defeated at Carmarthen. The party had always found it difficult to make progress in the Labour strongholds in South Wales, but at this election Plaid Cymru en- countered a strong Conservative revival in its own rural heartland.

After the election, when the government showed signs of departing from its campaign promise to allow the new fourth TV channel in Wales to be in Welsh, Gwynfor Evans, the Plaid Cymru President, fought a successful campaign to force the government to honour its pledge by threatening to fast to death. In its first year, the new Welsh language channel got 8 per cent of the Welsh TV audience. In its other activities, however, the party continued to experience hard times. Its main problem was an internal division between its left-wing and more traditional nationalists similar to that in the SNP. The establishment of a *National Left* group within the party in 1980 with a programme of 'decentralised Socialism' designed to oust Labour from its South Wales strongholds was countered in 1983 by the formation of the *Hydro group* by conservative nationalists. The Hydro group wanted the party to keep self-government for Wales in the forefront of its campaign and accordingly sought to reverse the 1981 amendment to the constitution which committed the party to the goal of a 'Socialist Wales'. The Hydro group blamed this Socialist trend for the poor showing of the party in the 1982 Gower by-election when the left-wing Plaid Cymru candidate lost his deposit. During 1982, Plaid Cymru also failed in its campaign to force the English customers of the Welsh Water Authority in the Midlands and North-West to pay more for their water. The party demanded increases worth £40 million from the English water authorities. If granted, such increases would have served both to reduce water rates for Welsh rate-payers (some of whom, the party claimed, were paying twice as much as their English counterparts) and to enable the Welsh Water Authority to make a profit on the export of one of the country's main natural resources. The party estimated that 10,000 households in Wales supported it by withholding water rates worth a total value of £4 million. But the campaign came to nothing. The government permitted a small increase only in the annual £1·3 million received for its supplies by the Welsh Water Authority and ruled that the prices charged by the authority should enable it to break even but not to make a profit.

In the early 1980s, the extremist fringe of Welsh nationalism drew public attention repeatedly with attacks upon English property and the English language. One Welsh language activist damaged and defaced road signs and destroyed television equipment of an estimated value of £28,000 in the cause. Even more seriously, there were frequent politically-motivated arson attacks on holiday homes of English people: between December 1979 and April 1984, over 70 such incidents took place in North Wales causing more than £400,000 worth of damage to property. Gravest of all were the terrorist activities claimed by a group called the Workers' Army of the Welsh Republic. These included the planting of explosive devices at the home of the Secretary of State for Wales, a Welsh Office building in Cardiff and the offices of the National Coal Board in Wales. Four members of the Welsh Socialist Republican Movement were tried for and acquitted of these offences in 1983.

In the 1983 general election, Plaid Cymru suffered further setbacks. Although its two MPs – Dafydd Wigley in Caernarfon and Dafydd Elis Thomas in Merionnyd Nant Conwy – retained their seats, the party failed to achieve its hoped-for gains in Carmarthen and Ynys Mon (Anglesey) and experienced a slight decline in its overall vote. Between its general election peak in February 1974 and 1983, its share of the Welsh vote declined. Serious problems remain for a party whose central concern – the protection and advancement of the Welsh language – divides rather than unites the nation.

Northern Ireland parties

Ulster politics are a law unto themselves. Parties and political issues in Northern Ireland bear virtually no resemblance to those throughout the rest of the United Kingdom. Nonetheless, the province remains part of the UK and, from 1983, sent seventeen MPs to Westminster. (Its previous representation was twelve). Its small parties merit consideration, therefore, along with the other minor parties.[8]

Ulster parties may be divided into three groupings according to the stand they take on three fundamental issues. These issues are the constitutional position of Northern Ireland within the UK; the rights of Catholics and especially the role of Protestants and Catholics within a devolved assembly in Ulster; and relationships with the Irish Republic. On these points of division, the principal political groupings are: Unionist; centrist (Alliance); and anti-partition (nationalist).

After the 1983 general election, the position with regard to seats in parliament was this: Unionist parties, fifteen; nationalist parties, two; non-sectarian Alliance, none. In terms of share of the vote, the two major Unionist groups (the Official Unionists led by James Molyneaux and the Democratic Unionists led by the Reverend Ian Paisley) had 54 per cent; the nationalists (the Social Democratic and Labour Party and Sinn Fein), 31·3 per cent; and the Alliance, a mere 8 per cent.

In 1972, the Westminster government abolished the Stormont parliament in Ulster, the former scene of Unionist operations, and imposed a system of direct rule upon the province which is still is existence. Thereafter, the British Government, which had for the previous half-century left Ulster largely to its own devices, became closely involved with its internal affairs. Most notably, it added to its responsibility for the maintenance of law and order a policy for the introduction of a devolved assembly based on power-sharing between Protestants and Catholics (and not, like the former Stormont parliament, on total Protestant domination). The imposition of direct rule transformed the political situation in Ulster. It had two important immediate effects. First, Unionist MPs, who had formerly been aligned with the Conservative Party and whose seats had been reckoned with the Conservative total in the House of Commons, broke this connection.

They felt that separate representation at Westminster was needed. The concerns of Ulster politics were thus imported directly into Westminster. In the 'no confidence' vote of 28 March 1979, Ulster MPs played a vital part in bringing down the Labour Government. Eight Ulster Unionists voted with the opposition parties, only two for the government. The SDLP and Independent Republican MPs abstained. Second, direct rule gave a further twist to the problem of achieving civil and constitutional rights for Ulster Catholics, which had begun under Terence O'Neill as Prime Minister in 1963 and continued with the Catholic civil rights movement in the late 1960s. The close involvement of the British Government in constitutional reform produced further pressure on the political representatives of both the Protestant and Catholic communities. The first electoral consequences of the Westminster policy of establishing an assembly based on power-sharing between Protestants and Catholics were seen in 1974. This review of political parties in Ulster accordingly begins with the general elections of that year, examining the three major groupings in turn.

The first point to note is that the official Unionist Party of Brian Faulkner, which endorsed the power-sharing policy of the British Government, virtually disintegrated in 1974. It was displaced by the United Ulster Unionist Council (UUUC), a coalition of Protestant Loyalist groups which came into being to contest the elections. In the previous four years most Unionists had moved away from the official Party, forming a series of splinter groups which came together under the broad umbrella of the UUUC to oppose power-sharing. These groups included Ian Paisley's Democratic Unionist Party (formed in 1970), William Craig's Vanguard Unionist Progressive Party (established in 1973) and a further group led by Harry West. In February 1974 eight West Unionists, two Vanguard Unionists and one Democratic Unionist were returned to parliament. In the October 1974 election, Harry West was defeated and the new parliamentary leader of his group became J.Molyneaux. In this election, UUUC anti-power-sharing candidates won ten of the twelve Ulster seats.

The other Northern Ireland party represented at Westminster is the Social Democratic and Labour Party (SDLP). Formed in 1970 in the aftermath of the Civil Rights campaign, under the leadership of Gerry Fitt, who won West Belfast, it had become the leading Catholic party by 1974. It aims at the achievement of Socialism as well as the abolition of discrimination against Catholics in Ulster. It is anti-partition, wanting a united Ireland based on the consent of the majority. This effectively limits its appeal to Catholics despite its otherwise non-sectarian stance. The remaining Ulster seat in October 1974 (Fermanagh and Tyrone) was won by an independent Republican, M.F. Maguire. The only other party with an appeal to a significant proportion of voters at these elections was the Alliance. It supports participation in government by both Protestants and Catholics, wants equal opportunities for all citizens and whilst favouring the maintenance of the Union also advocates closer relations with the Irish Republic. But its balanced, non-sectarian programme failed to win any seats in 1974.

The main party struggle within Northern Ireland since 1972 has been for the control of the Ulster Unionist Party. All Unionists stand for the maintenance of the constitutional link between Northern Ireland and the UK: the dispute has been over the terms on which that link can and should be maintained. The Unionists withdrew from Faulkner's official Unionist Party because they did not want to share power with Catholics; they equate the Union with Great Britain and the maintenance of Protestant ascendancy and value it also as a bulwark against a united Ireland dominated by Dublin. But this does not mean that Ulster Unionism will accept any policy that a British Government might try to impose, particularly if it extends political, social and economic opportunities for Catholics in Northern Ireland. Groups like those led by Paisley and Craig wanted to retain the British link *and* go their own political way within Northern Ireland. They demand the restoration of Stormont and the cession of control of internal security arrangements. Paisley's organisation, the Democratic Unionist Party, is a populist party which builds on Protestant fears of a Catholic religious and political take-over of Ulster. Its leader is prepared to ally with extra-parliamentary paramilitary organisations. In May 1977 his participation in a Protestant strike broke the UUUC. James Molyneaux withdrew the Official Unionists from the coalition, denouncing the DUP for aiming ultimately at independence for

Northern Ireland. Political events in the decade or so after 1972 showed, however, how little Ulster Unionism in general was prepared to concede on the major political and constitutional questions. In many ways, it was merely a political arm of the Orange Order, a religious organisation which had been associated with most of the major riots in Ulster since the 1830s. Membership of this fiercely intolerant Protestant Order remained virtually a precondition for entry into the party.

The 1979 general election produced little change in the politics of the province. Ten Unionist MPs were again returned, together with Gerry Fitt (SDLP) and M.F.Maguire (Independent Republican); or, to put matters slightly differently, ten Protestant MPs and two Roman Catholics. The ultimate goal for Unionists remained the restoration of Stormont, but within the group, attitudes to the major UK parties differed. The official Unionists, led by James Molyneaux, thought that Labour was more likely than the Conservatives to return to devolved government in Northern Ireland, although local government powers were a probable interim stage. Their main rivals, the Democratic Unionist Party, criticised official Unionists for having kept Labour in power at the expense of pro-Stormont interests and for their illogicality in first helping to defeat the Labour Government and then arguing that Labour had more to offer than the Conservatives. The Democratic Unionists did well at the election, gaining two seats, Belfast East and Belfast North, from the official Unionists.

In the 1983 general election, Unionists won fifteen of the seats (Official Unionists eleven, Democratic Unionists three with one Popular Unionist). The major new development was the growing strength of Sinn Fein (SF), the political wing of the IRA, which competed with the SDLP for Catholic votes. Although John Hume beat off the SF challenge in Foyle, Gerry Fitt lost his West Belfast constituency to the Sinn Fein leader, Gerry Adams. In order to allow Gerry Adams to take his seat at Westminster, the British Government had to lift the exclusion order under the Prevention of Terrorism Act which banned him from travelling to Britain. Sinn Fein narrowly failed to win a second seat but easily exceeded the target of 90,000 votes it had set itself, gaining 13·4 per cent of the total vote. By contrast, the SDLP slipped back, winning a 17·9 per cent share of the poll compared with 19·7 per cent in 1979.

The extreme right

The National Front is the leading party on the extreme right in Britain (even if, in this case, the term 'Britain' is something of a misnomer since the party has never achieved any significant success outside England). It was founded in 1967 by a merger between the League of Empire Loyalists (1954), the British National Party (1960) and part of the Racial Preservation Society (1964). When the Greater Britain Movement disbanded in 1967, many ex-members also went on to join the Front and its leader, John Tyndall, later became the Front's chairman. His book *Six Principles of British Nationalism* (1966) expresses the political beliefs of the movement and became required reading for members. These are: strong, firm government based on popular consent which unleashes rather than paralyses British genius; the re-emergence of Britain as a world power through a new white Commonwealth; economic nationalism based on the transformation of the Commonwealth into a self-sufficient enclosed economic system; the preservation of the British race by means of resistance to racial integration and the maintenance of racial separateness; the creation of a government of the national will rising above party and class and based on a genuine mass movement; and, finally, a programme of complete national moral regeneration, involving the prosecution of those who promote art, literature and entertainment which endangers public standards, together with a stress on smartness and discipline in national life.[9]

Its manifesto in the 1979 general election provides further evidence of its extreme right-wing ideas. Entitled *It's Our Country – Let's Win It Back* it called for the repatriation of blacks and the restriction of foreign aid to countries which granted favours such as the repatriation of their nationals living in Britain. At a press conference to launch the manifesto, its chairman, John Tyndall, stated that the NF thought that it was necessary 'to do something about the coloureds here and their potential increase'. Its manifesto declared that, on coming to office, the Front would place 'all coloured immigrants and their offspring on a register of persons liable to be required eventually to leave this country'. In cases of mixed marriage, the white partner would normally be expected to leave Britain with his or her spouse. The NF also called for Britain to withdraw from the Common Market, the development of friendly ties with South Africa and a realignment in foreign policy from Israel towards the Arab states. The Front would also abolish comprehensive schools and introduce profit-sharing. It dislikes the United Nations and is violently anti-communist. The NF, then, is a nationalist party which increasingly has made a racialist appeal. In 1975 its journal *Spearhead* contended that 'racialism is the only scientific and logical basis of nationalism' and suggested that 'racial interbreeding' could destroy the 'British nation'. The Front blames the 'black and brown aliens' for high unemployment, and, in certain areas, for poor housing, education and welfare services. In the mid-1970s it constituted a particular challenge in inner-city areas where Labour Party constituency organisation was in decay and many voters, especially young, white working-class people, perhaps felt betrayed by Labour's social policies. In October 1974 its strategy was to concentrate its candidates in constituencies containing coloured immigrants and it did best in the East End of London, where it got 6·2 per cent of the vote in thirteen Labour-held seats. In the GLC elections in 1977 the Front demanded the removal of coloured immigrants from waiting lists for council housing and the segregation of immigrants' children from the rest in schools. In Scotland, it aimed to expose the alleged inconsistency of SNP nationalism which was hostile to England but not to coloured people, being prepared to allow Asians into Scotland.

The internal politics of the NF have been disorderly, marked by faction fights, leadership struggles and splits. In its first thirteen years, the leadership changed hands several times, from A.K.Chesterton (1967–1970) to John O'Brien (1970–1972) to John Tyndall (1972–1974 and 1975–1980) while Kingsley Read was briefly leader in 1974 and Andrew Brons succeeded Tyndall as Chairman in 1980. The personality, past career and aspirations of Tyndall, in fact, were at the heart of these intra-party feuds. Initially excluded from the party for his 'neo-Nazi' background, his alleged infiltration of the Front in 1972 led to the departure of

John O'Brien. In the mid-1970s a fierce struggle took place between his group and the 'Populists', during which Tyndall was sacked from the chairmanship and nearly expelled from the party a year later. Once again, however, the power struggle led to his principal opponent quitting the party; Kingsley Read left, taking 3,000 NF members with him, to form a new rival group, the National Party, which, however, collapsed in 1977. Tyndall's continued effort to secure his own power by transforming the NF constitution into an 'elective dictatorship' led to a third split in 1979–1980. On that occasion, Andrew Fountaine, a leader of the opposition to Tyndall, lost his place on the executive, and immediately left to form a splinter group, the National Front Constitutional Movement. Shortly afterwards, Anthony Reed Herbert led another faction out of the Front to form the British Democratic Party. The most severe internal crisis yet faced by the NF ended with Tyndall's own resignation after he had failed to persuade the Directorate to call an extraordinary general meeting of the party to consider his request for enlarged constitutional powers. He went on to form the New National Front, leaving his former organisation in confusion. Martin Webster, the NF National Activities organiser, now became its leading figure. In the early 1980s, a series of court cases kept the Front in the public eye. These involved Webster himself (on public order offences and a libel action concerning Peter Hain) and Joseph Pearce, the editor of *Bulldog*, the NF youth paper, who was convicted of incitement to racial hatred.

The NF has followed the classic 'two-track' strategy of parties of the extreme right. It uses the tactics of 'legality', appealing for support at elections just like liberal-democratic parties whilst at the same time maintaining its covert links with small neo-Nazi groups in Britain and abroad. In Britain, the most important of these groups is the *British Movement*, a virulently anti-semitic organisation with a strong para-military side which was formed by another prominent post-war Nazi, Colin Jordan, in 1968. This double strategy explains much about the National Front. On the one hand, it is a 'protest' party similar in function, although not in ideology and policy, to the Liberals or the Welsh and Scottish nationalists. It is against both of the major parties and against the two-party system. In this sense, its role has been to provide some white voters who felt that their interests had been abandoned by the major parties with a means of registering their hostility to coloured people.[10] But the Front is also an anti-democratic organisation whose 'demos' and marches involving its youthful combat-jacketed militants are more than a device to gain publicity for a party without parliamentary representation. Rather they serve to express and reinforce its commitment to an anti-rational politics of 'toughness' and violent self-assertion, to the methods of fists and boots rather than peaceful persuasion. They are intended as proofs of its determination to make its views prevail against all opponents.

The NF has achieved little success in national elections. During its most successful phase – in the mid-1970s – it concentrated on the exploitation of public concern over coloured immigration. It first began to receive serious attention in 1973 when, in the aftermath of the issue caused by the entry of the Ugandan Asians expelled by Idi Amin, Martin Webster received over 16 per cent of the vote in a by-election at West Bromwich. In the 1974 general elections it displaced the Communist Party as Britain's fourth party. None of the fifty-four and ninety NF candidates at the respective elections was returned to parliament but it gained over 76,000 votes in February and more than 113,000 in October. Two years later, the Front won an average 8·9 per cent of the vote in the local election seats it contested, polling especially well at Leicester where it received over 44,000 votes, 18 per cent of the total vote. In May 1977 the party contested all but one of the ninety-two Greater London Council seats, beat the Liberals into fourth place in about one-third of the seats and gained 120,000 votes. In the boroughs of Hackney, Newham and Tower Hamlets it polled over 10 per cent of the vote.

In the late 1970s and early 1980s, weakened by its own internal feuds, the National Front failed to maintain its earlier momentum. On the streets, it encountered increasing resistance, much of it organised by the Anti-Nazi League, in which the extreme left activists were prominent. Membership declined[11] and even though the party ambitiously ran over 300 candidates in the 1979 general election, its vote rose by little over one-third to 191,267, a mere 0·6 per cent of the total vote.

The fragmentation, electoral weakness and increasing violence of the extreme right are the main themes of the early 1980s. Local election results in May 1981 were disastrous. Three groups, the National Front, New National Front and Constitutional Movement contested the GLC elections, but achieved minute percentages of the vote. Candidates from the Constitutional Movement, the British Movement and the British Democratic Party did equally badly in local elections elsewhere.[12] In the 1983 general election, the National Front (sixty) and the British National Party (fifty-three) put forward candidates for the extreme right. Neither group had any success: the NF got 27,065 votes at an average of 1·1 per cent candidate; the BNP, now led by Tyndall, received only 14,621 votes at an average of 0·6 per cent candidate.[13] The Front had not recaptured its momentum of the mid-1970s; nor had any of its extreme nationalist rivals been able to do so. Meanwhile, as the electoral challenge collapsed, violent racial attacks in the streets increased, fomented by the anti-blacks and anti-Jewish propaganda of the extreme right.

The extreme left

Although under challenge from other – especially Trotskyist – groups in the 1970s, the Communist Party of Great Britain (CPGB) remains the leading far left group. It was formed in 1920 from the British Socialist Party and the Socialist Labour Party (the left wing of the Independent Labour Party) and sees itself as the bearer of true socialist ideas in a broad coalition with the left in the Labour Party and in the trade unions. It claims that the Labour Party as a whole has betrayed the working class and the Socialist movement by coming to terms with capitalism in the guise of a 'mixed economy'. The CPGB adopts the classical Marxist view that capitalism is in crisis. It opposes workers' representation on boards of management as 'class collaboration' and advocates nationalisation of land, insurance companies, banks and all productive enterprises, although it would allow homes and personal belongings to remain in private hands. The Party would abolish the House of Lords, but otherwise its brand of Socialism would make concessions to the British way of life: it would permit habeas corpus, an independent judiciary, a plurality of parties and personal freedoms to remain.[14] In *The British Road to Socialism* (1976), the first revision of its programme since 1968, the Party called for British withdrawal from the EEC and NATO and for the abandonment of the Social Contract and the restoration of collective bargaining. Its 1979 manifesto advocated the restoration of free collective bargaining together with a minimum wage of £60 per week, full guarantees of the right to strike and peaceful picketing, a 35-hour week, more money for the regions, a six-month price freeze, the abolition of VAT, the imposition of purchase tax on luxuries, and subsidised food, public transport and rents.

The CPGB experienced its period of greatest success in the 1940s but has suffered steady erosion of its position since that time. The circulation of its newspaper, the *Morning Star*, whose predecessor the *Daily Worker* (established 1930) sold 122,000 copies in 1947, had declined to about 30,000 in 1984. Without the bulk order for a daily 15,000 copies from the Soviet Union, which brings in an annual £1 million, the position would be much worse. Membership also is falling: it stood at 56,000 in 1942 but was down to 13,500 in 1984, a more than fourfold decrease. In addition, the CPGB attracts minute and diminishing support at elections. In 1945 it polled over 100,000 votes and returned two MPs, but it has not managed to match this subsequently. In the thirty-five years after 1950, the party failed to elect another MP, and attracted more than 50,000 votes in only two elections (1950 itself and 1966). After February 1974, when it received just over 30,000 votes, its support in general elections has declined even further and it polled only 11,606 votes in 1983. Its thirty-five candidates averaged a mere 0·8 per cent of the vote. Faced with this situation, the CPGB has shown signs of focusing more upon its industrial than its parliamentary strategy, concentrating on gaining influence through the trade unions. But its ultimate goal remains obviously political – the achievement of what it sees as a genuinely Socialist society in Britain.

The party's highest policy-making body is the National Congress. This body elects a National Executive Committee, which meets twice every month and is responsible for policy between Congresses. The party acquired a new General Secretary in 1975 when Gordon McLennan replaced John Gollan, who had held the office since 1956. Trade unions such as the engineering, transport and construction workers have been particularly strongly represented at recent congresses but many other unions, including the mineworkers, electricians, teachers, higher education teachers, students and journalists, regularly send delegates. Some CPGB members have achieved prominence both in individual unions and on the General Council of the TUC: Ken Gill of the technicians' union (TASS) and Mick McGahey of the miners (NUM) are the leading examples.

In the late 1970s and early 1980s, the CPGB underwent severe internal strains as a consequence of its doctrinal trimming. It dissociated itself from its former automatic support for the USSR and moved towards a gradualist, Eurocommunist position. But, in doing so, the party came under fire from pro-Soviet hardliners. In 1977, the new policy proposed in *The British Road to Socialism* caused considerable controversy at Congress and was rejected by a Stalinist splinter group whose members admired the Soviet Union. Led by Sid French, the group left the CPGB to form the New Communist Party. It had about 800 members in 1979 and its newspaper, the *New Worker*, claimed 4,000 readers. Violent dissension broke out again at the 1983 Congress. Once more, the Eurocommunist leadership came under attack from a pro-Soviet traditionalist element, led this time by the party's former industrial organiser and current industrial correspondent of the *Morning Star*, Mick Costello. The critics condemned the leadership on two main grounds: firstly, for abandoning the class struggle in industry in its search for a broader political alliance involving other radical groups as well as manual workers; and secondly, for disapproving of the Soviet occupation of Afghanistan and of the imposition of martial law in Poland. This phase of the controversy ended in a heavy defeat for the pro-Soviet opposition. Seven of the critics, including the editor of the *Morning Star*, Tony Chater, his deputy editor, David Whitfield, and Costello himself, lost their seats on the Executive Committee. Three members were subsequently expelled for backing the pro-Soviet faction at Congress. The struggle then shifted to the *Morning Star*, which had become a stronghold of the dissentients. The victorious CPGB Executive called for the resignation of its editor and deputy-editor and their replacement by two of its nominees. However, the *Morning Star* was not under the direct control of the party, a factor which gravely weakened the position of the Executive on this occasion. In fact, the paper was run by a cooperative, the People's Press Printing Society, and consequently, in order to make its views prevail, the CPGB leadership had to get a majority on the twelve-strong management committee of the PPPS. This it failed to do in June 1984, when hardliners maintained their control by a 10–2 majority. But neither did the paper's editor win a vote of confidence in his editorship. The rift between the more 'liberal' Eurocommunists and the conservative pro-Soviet faction seemed set to continue.

Beginning in the late 1960s, other far left groups have gained in importance.[15] When considered together with the emergence of far right groups, this trend represents a significant relative increase in the importance of anti-system politics. These groups reject and ultimately wish to destroy the parliamentary system, even if some of them are prepared to use the system for their own purposes by, for example, running candidates in elections. The leading Trotskyist groups are the Workers' Revolutionary Party (WRP), the International Marxist Group (IMG), and the Militant tendency. Led by Gerry Healy, the WRP is the most fundamentalist of these groups, lashing out periodically at fellow-Trotskyists as well as the mainstream Labour Party for their various acts of 'betrayal'. It supports the IRA and, in international politics, the Libyan leader, Colonel Gadaffi and the Palestine Liberation Organisation (PLO). Like the CPGB, it stresses the industrial side of its activities and has established the All Trade Union Alliance movement for that purpose. It runs two journals, a daily paper, *Newsline*, and in 1980 had about 3,000 members. In elections, it is even less successful than the CPGB. In 1983, its twenty candidates polled only 3,643 votes between them, averaging a mere 0·4 per cent each. The IMG is the British section of the United Secretariat of the Fourth International (The fourth international was set up by Trotsky in 1938 to organise opposition to fascism better than the third international had done). It was formed in 1965 and, like the WRP, in its early days recruited many ex-members of the Communist Party who had resigned over Soviet action in Hungary in 1956. The IMG is a small group with a membership of about 800 in 1978. But it contains several prominent Marxist intellectuals, notably Tariq Ali, Robin Blackburn and Ernest Mandel, and its publications – *Black Dwarf* and *Red Mole* in the 1970s and now *Socialist Challenge* – reach considerable numbers on the left. Seeking to detach the support of the working class from the Labour Party, the IMG called for a broad alliance on the left – Socialist Unity – in the late 1970s; its candidate under this banner won 3·4 per cent of the vote in the Ladywood by-election in 1977. The leader of Militant tendency, Ted Grant, was formerly a member of the Revolutionary Communist Party with Gerry Healy, subsequently of the WRP, and Tony Cliff, later of the Socialist Workers' Party. When the Revolutionary Communist Party broke up after 1947, Grant became leader of the Revolutionary Socialist League (RSL): it was the RSL's publication *Socialist Fight* which became *Militant* in 1963. The tendency, the least respected theoretically but the most influential practically of the Trotskyist sects, came into existence, it is believed, in the early 1960s when the RSL submerged in the interests of 'entryism'. 'Entryism', as practised by the revolutionary left, involves the infiltration of the mainstream Labour Party for three purposes: to influence its policy in a more hardline Socialist direction; to win converts to its cause among Labour supporters; and to provoke division and ultimately a split in the party from which it might benefit. This political strategy is by no means a new one on the left and Militant tendency is certainly not alone in practising it. But in the 1970s and early 1980s, it has been the most successful leftist sect in the use of this tactic. It gained control of the Executive Committee of the Labour Party Young Socialists in 1970 and later turned its attention with some success to increasing its influence in constituency Labour parties. (See pp. 50–51 for an account of the debate within the Labour Party unleashed by its activities in the late 1970s). One of the most successful centres of operation is Liverpool. There in 1984, Militant had supporters in influential Labour Party positions in most of the thirty-three wards; the President of the District Labour Party, Tony Mulhearn, is a Militant sympathiser; and fifteen of the fifty Labour councillors, including the Deputy Leader of the Council, are members of Militant. Estimates of its national membership vary but in the early 1980s this may have been as high as 3,500, which figure, if accurate, would have made Militant the largest far left group in Britain.

Finally, no survey of the extreme left would be complete without mention of the Socialist Workers' Party (SWP). Like the other small Marxist sects, the deeper origins of the SWP lie in the break-up of the Revolutionary Communist Party after 1947. More specifically it began in 1976 when the International Socialists (1962) changed their name to the Socialist Workers' Party. The party – which counts among its most prominent adherents, Tony Cliff, Paul Foot and Mike Kidron, the owner of Pluto Press – adopts a strategy of stimulating industrial militancy rather than 'entryism'. It does run parliamentary candidates for publicity purposes but from the late 1970s has made a far greater impact by leading aggressive right to work and anti-racism campaigns. It diagnoses the hold of Labour Party 'reformism' on the working class as weak and seeks to win its support for a revolutionary alternative. Despite claims of a circulation of 30,000, its paper the *Socialist Worker* in fact sold under 14,000 copies in 1978.[16] After its activity in the Anti-Nazi League and among the Asian communities, its membership rose to about 5,000 in 1980.

The Ecology Party
Founded in 1973, the Ecology Party stands for the protection of the environment. Its causes are those which have frequently hit the headlines in the 1980s – for example, the protests against acid rain from the dirty burning of coal, against lead in petrol, against the dumping of nuclear waste, and, above all, against the dangers of nuclear holocaust. Its 1983 general election manifesto *Politics for Life* called for unilateral disarmament; work for all based on self-reliance and renewable resources; changes in farm methods; an equal society; and help for the Third World. In short, the party exists to draw attention to and, if possible, reverse those industrial and agricultural practices in contemporary societies which place the future of humanity in jeopardy by polluting and destroying the environment. These practices are often built into the whole way of life of modern people. Thus, the climatic balance in Britain is subject to long-term alteration by emissions of carbon dioxide which warm the atmosphere of the earth; and in turn, climatic change could adversely affect the food supply. The party would agree with a British report (1983) of the World Conservation Strategy that what is needed are policies designed 'to

find a means of satisfying genuine human needs on a pattern compatible with the healthy survival of the biosphere'.

The party entered the 1983 election campaign with high hopes of improving its achievement in 1979 when its fifty-three candidates won an average 1·5 per cent of the poll in the seats contested. Despite a considerable drop in its 1981 membership of 8,000 in the following two years as a result of the formation of the SDP, the party still had 4,500 members organised in 250 branches and an able co-chairman in Jonathan Porritt. It had the electoral backing of Women for Life on Earth, the main organisation at women-only peace camps such as Greenham Common. Public opinion, moreover, seemed to be favourable. In Britain, a MORI poll in January 1983 showed quite high levels of public concern about pollution and resource depletion. 25 per cent of respondents placed pollution higher than unemployment, inflation and law and order as the top priority to be tackled; 58 per cent were prepared to support a penny in the pound on income tax to finance effective measures to reduce resource-waste. On the continent, 'green' parties had had their successes: 'green' MPs sat in several national parliaments as well as in the European parliament; and in West Germany, led by Petra Kelly, they had gained twenty-seven seats on a 5·6 per cent share of the poll earlier in 1983. Finally, as part of the wider 'green' movement, the Ecology Party might hope to appeal to members of such kindred groups as Friends of the Earth and Greenpeace as well as some of the 3 million who belong to conservation societies but not to any of the other political parties. In the months before the election, well-attended 'Green Rallies' addressed by Des Wilson, chairman of the campaign for lead-free air, Graham Searle, Chairman of the Stop Sizewell-B campaign, and Joan Ruddock, chairperson of CND, were held in London, Leeds and Bristol.

The election result was disappointing for the party. Its 108 candidates gained only 54,299 votes, a mere 1 per cent of the poll in the seats fought.[17] The party might no longer be thought of as 'a bunch of woolly-hatted, woolly-headed lentil-stirrers', the dismissive phrase often used about it in the 1970s. Its efforts along with those of other 'green' organisations had helped to produce more favourable public attitudes towards conservation of energy supplies, working with natural processes and protection of other species. Moreover, by October 1984, membership was increasing again, and had reached 6,500. But three factors worked against it. Firstly, other parties were also becoming educated in environmental matters, and included these themes in their addresses and manifestoes. Second, the party was held back by its single issue appeal. Finally, like other minor parties, it tended to suffer from lack of credibility: people would not vote for it because they thought it had little chance even of getting a handful of MPs. And without proportional representation, this would seem to be the case.

5 Pressure Groups

During the 1960s and 1970s, British Governments of both political complexions were anxious to govern with the consent of the major sectional groupings. Two excellent examples of pressure group activity in that period of 'corporatist' government are the initiative on prices taken by the Confederation of British Industry (CBI) in 1971 and the blocking by the Trades Union Congress (TUC) of Labour's proposed legislation in 1969. Campaigning groups in the field of social policy such as Child Poverty Action, the Disablement Income Group and Shelter also emerged in that period and their activities in representing the interests of otherwise powerless sections of the community were seen as valuably complementary to the political parties in a pluralist society. After 1979, however, the political climate changed. Conservative Governments had a policy of keeping organised interests at arm's length and, in the case of the trade unions, of reducing their privileges. In addition, campaigning welfare groups gained much less sympathy from governments keeping a fierce grip on health, housing and educational spending. Now sectional and campaigning groups' characteristic activities of behind-the-scenes persuasion and close contact with government remain very important. But in the 1980s, as parliamentary opposition to the government's policies weakened, and public anxiety on such issues as international tension and large-scale unemployment increased, national attention focused on two public protest campaigns arising out of these concerns. The groups at the centre of these campaigns were the Campaign for Nuclear Disarmament (CND) and the National Union of Mine-workers (NUM). Public campaigning, of course, is by no means a new strategy. What was novel about the situation was the large extent to which the central democratic function of political opposition had come to be located in extra-parliamentary pressure groups. This is the justification for beginning this chapter with these campaigns against nuclear weapons and for the preservation of jobs in mining and in the British economy generally.

The Campaign for Nuclear Disarmament (CND) is the leading organisation in a peace movement which had over a quarter of a million supporters by 1982.[1] It grew very rapidly after 1978 against a threatening sequence of world events. East-West tension increased sharply after the Russian invasion of Afghanistan in 1979 and the establishment of a military government in Poland in 1981. It was accompanied by a rapid growth of nuclear arsenals and defence spending in general in the West in the late 1970s and early 1980s. The modernisation of nuclear weaponry at this time was of special significance to the upsurge of the peace movement. In December 1979 NATO decided to up-date its theatre nuclear weapons, which involved the introduction of Cruise and Pershing missiles into several European countries from the end of 1983. In March 1980, the British Government announced that it would accept 160 Cruise Missiles to be based at Greenham Common in Berkshire and at Molesworth in Cambridgeshire. In doing so, it was signalling its agreement with the NATO belief that Soviet SS 20s posed an intensified nuclear threat that had to be countered. At the same time, the government indicated its intention to replace Britain's ageing Polaris submarine fleet with a new Trident submarine-launched missile in the 1990s.

CND aims at a neutralist Britain which is no longer part of NATO and which has renounced its nuclear weapons. It argues that, far from acting as a deterrent, Britain's nuclear weapons increase the probability of a war in which the numbers dying would be on an unparalleled scale. It cites scientific opinion that a 220-megaton attack would be followed by months of darkness at noon and an Ice Age in which survivors of the initial blast would either freeze or starve to death. Renunciation of nuclear weapons by the UK, it maintains, would break the 'log jam' in which no power dare take the first step towards disarmament. Second, it points out that the new generation of nuclear weapons installed in Britain and Europe in 1983–4 have far greater strike capacity than previous nuclear weapons. When set alongside existing weapons, they give NATO the nuclear advantage over the

Warsaw Pact, and therefore de-stabilise the situation. European security lies not in such continuing escalation but in the abandonment of nuclear weapons by NATO and the Warsaw Pact and the transformation of the continent from Poland to Portugal into a 'nuclear-free zone'. Finally, CND disagrees with the official statement that the use of nuclear weapons will be a matter of joint British-American decision; rather, in its view, it will be made by the Americans alone. The government riposted to these arguments in late 1982 and early 1983 with a strong campaign of speeches by leading Ministers led by the Defence Secretary, Michael Heseltine. The government maintained that the possession of nuclear weapons by the West *had* served as a deterrent and had played the key role in keeping world peace in the post-war period. Without them, Britain, Western Europe and the United States would be exposed to nuclear blackmail (as China had been before she got the bomb) or invasion (like Afghanistan) or the threat of it (like Poland). The British nuclear deterrent strengthened European defence, making its military response more difficult to predict than if it depended on the United States alone. Moreover, it meant Europe could be defended if circumstances arose in which the United States was unprepared to risk its own cities in order to protect Europe. In addition, Polaris, and, in the future, Trident, were guarantees against a nuclear threat to Britain as well as being a source of international political influence.

Lacking resources in demand by government and never likely to convert government directly, CND success has to be measured in terms of its impact on public opinion. As it had done during the earlier phase of its existence in 1960, CND captured the Labour Party for unilateralism. It also won the support of the Ecology Party and grass-roots Liberals (but not the Liberal leadership or the SDP). Between 1982 and 1984, according to the polls, between one-fifth and one-quarter of the public supported unilateral renunciation of nuclear weapons and about half was opposed to British acceptance of Cruise missiles. CND's own support mounted rapidly: by April 1983, it had 54,000 members and employed twenty-eight full-time staff. The names of its leaders, Mrs Joan Ruddock and Monsignor Bruce Kent, were household words. Just over a year later (November 1984), membership had doubled to 110,000. Moreover, the peace movement of which CND was a part was much broader still, with an estimated membership of slightly over 300,000 in December, 1983. After April 1980, the European Nuclear Disarmament group (END) helped to establish contacts between British and European unilateralists. The World Disarmament Campaign (WDC) has a multilateralist approach, but is undeniably part of the peace movement. In addition, there are literally hundreds of peace groups, drawing all sections for society into the movement – churches, trade unions, parties, local authorities, and, with particular intensity, since their protest began on 12 December, 1982, the Greenham Common women.

However, by the beginning of 1985, despite its wide appeal, CND had not made the most of its potential. Britons were anxious about the military implications of Cruise and Trident and about the cost of Trident (estimated at over £10 billion in December 1984) but the majority were not unilateralist. The best strategy in the circumstances would have been to concentrate its campaign on such issues as resistance to Cruise and Trident, a strategy of minimum deterrence, mutual freeze and the unacceptability of constantly rising costs. In the event, it came to be associated in the public mind with one-sided calls for the nuclear disarmament of the West. CND was weakened by the breadth of the movement, which encompassed a wide spectrum of opinion from the extreme left to Christian pacifism, and by the loose decentralisation of its decision-making structure. At its 1984 Conference, a proposal that CND launch a full-scale criticism of Soviet nuclear weapons was evaded. Its chairperson Joan Ruddock explained that the motion which asked for a much higher priority to be given to anti-Soviet demonstrations would divide the movement: hence, it had been decided not to put it.

The Miners' Strike 1984–5. On 1 March 1984, the decision to close Cortonwood pit in Yorkshire was communicated to area officials of the National Union of Mineworkers (NUM) by the area manager of the National Coal Board. The pit was losing £20 per tonne, was 'uneconomic' and would consequently have to close in five weeks' time. The decision was made against a background of increasing mistrust between the NUM and the NCB over pit closures, which had intensified after the appointment of Ian McGregor as Chairman of the Board in September 1983. The NUM leadership feared that he had been brought in to 'do a hatchet job' on the industry. Within five days of the Cortonwood announcement, their worst fears seemed to be confirmed. In 1984, the NCB told mining union leaders it planned to reduce output by 4 million tonnes, involving the closure of twenty pits and the loss of 20,000 jobs. The unions responded swiftly. By 12 March, the majority of Britain's 180,000 miners were out on strike.[2]

The national impact of the strike was immense. By the end of 1984, it was still in progress having been in existence for just under nine months and nearly 300 days. Nor was the end in sight. It was already the longest national stoppage in trade union history. Moreover, in late October it had lasted longer than the lock-out of 1926 and resulted in the loss of more working days than any industrial dispute for over half a century. It had placed both courts and police under heavy strain. Between 13 March and 11 December, 7,314 people were charged with offences in the dispute and 3,040 were convicted; more than 3,000 cases waited to be dealt with – a huge backlog. In the first nine months of the strike, hundreds of police, strikers and working miners were injured. Directly or indirectly, the strike was responsible for over a dozen deaths. By early November, the economic costs of the strike were also severe. It was estimated to have cost each striking miner £5,500 in lost wages and the Coal Board £2 billion (two million millions) in lost production. It had cost the nation an additional £1 billion owing to its adverse effects on the electricity industry and the railways, the additional burden of social security benefits, policing and lost income tax revenue. In mid-December the government calculated policing costs alone at £103 million. Whatever its outcome, a more dramatic example of sectional pressure group activity would be very hard to find. How had it come about?

A major reason lies in the unusually combative and uncompromising nature of the Prime Minister and the President of the NUM. In 1972 and 1974, Conservative Governments had been defeated by miners' strikes and again in 1981 the government backed down quickly when faced by a strike on pit closures, Mrs

Thatcher's only significant defeat by a trade union. On that occasion coal stocks were low and the miners had widespread support from other unions. The Conservatives were unready to face down a major strike. However, an internal party report by Nicholas Ridley in 1978 advised them how to prepare for such an event by building up coal stocks and alternative energy supplies for the power stations, reducing social security benefits for strikers, arming employers with new civil law sanctions and getting the police to work out better national coordination to minimise the effects of 'flying pickets'. Well-organised picketing outside the Saltley power station had paved the way for the success of the 1972 strike. After the 1983 general election, the Conservative Government both expected and were prepared for a trial of strength with the miners. They were confronted by an NUM under the determined left-wing leadership of Arthur Scargill and Mick McGahey. In the 1960s and 1970s, the generally right-wing leadership of the union had had to accept huge job losses as demand for coal declined and the industry contracted. In 1968 alone, fifty-five collieries were closed and 55,000 jobs were lost, nearly three times the number proposed for 1984. In the 1980s, the union's resistance hardened. But, in the context of world economic recession and deteriorating morale in the Labour movement, the miners voted against strike action on three occasions between 1981 and 1984 – on pay (January 1982), pay and closures (October 1982) and closures (March 1983). The NUM President wanted to oppose closures within the context of a much broader campaign by the whole Labour movement against the policies of the Conservative Government. But he had to proceed cautiously and in particular avoid another defeat on a national ballot that would have been a further severe blow to his standing as leader.

In fact, the strike began without a national ballot. Whereas Rule 43 of the NUM Rule Book lays down that a national strike cannot be undertaken without a ballot of the members, Rule 41 provides that Areas can take industrial action short of a strike providing their actions are sanctioned at national level. The NUM proceeded on these lines.[3] Area by area stoppages were endorsed by a Conference in May. Calls by right-wingers on the NUM Executive for a national ballot were defeated. In the early weeks of the strike, the left consistently outmanoeuvred the right. It argued that jobs were too important a matter to vote on. But the failure to hold a national ballot gave a strong propaganda card to the government. Moreover, opinion polls taken between March and July indicated that a clear majority of miners favoured strike action. The NUM may also have made a mistake in picketing the Nottinghamshire coalfield – a traditionally moderate area – before the Nottinghamshire miners had balloted. Whether this was a decisive factor in leading to the anti-strike vote of 3:1 is debatable, but the action was resented. It is certain that continuing production by the Nottingham area was a grave source of weakness in the strike. It helped maintain coal stocks and it made it difficult for the NUM to persuade other trade unions to assist them.

During the late spring and early summer, a fierce struggle took place between pickets and police. The struggle was about the capacity of the striking miners to prevent the major industrial customers of the NCB like British Steel receiving their coal supplies and about whether they could stop working miners getting in to work. A police operation on an unprecedented scale was launched to ensure they failed in these objectives. Police activity was coordinated from the National Reporting Centre at New Scotland Yard and thousands of extra police were drafted into the Yorkshire and East Midlands coalfields. By autumn the picture was clearer. The miners would find it hard to win their strike unless there was an exceptionally severe winter (and perhaps not even then); a strike by NACODS, the pit deputies' union (which would close all the pits); or considerable support from other unions (especially the electricity, steel and transport workers). By early January 1985, none of these things had happened. The winter had been relatively mild; a NACODS strike had flared briefly (and for the Coal Board and government dangerously) in mid-October but had been quickly settled; and the TUC, whilst promising support in August, had produced little in the way of positive action. Key unions (electricity, electrical engineering and steel) refused to help, and the activities of the rail and seamen's unions, which did give assistance, were offset by the willingness of transport workers to work overtime to beat the ban on the movement of coal. Moreover, coalfield 'violence' had tended to dominate public discussion at the expense of other issues raised by the strike such as the role of coal in future national energy policy, the fate of mining communities when pits closed and even the definition of an 'uneconomic' pit. Despite some anxieties on these issues expressed in speeches and in the columns of 'quality' newspapers by 'moderate' opinion, especially churchmen and academics, the battle for public opinion was not being won by the miners.

At the end of 1984, both the finish and the outcome of the strike were unforeseeable. But the NUM wore an increasingly beleaguered look. A very slow drift back to work had begun. Moreover, although in many areas the strike remained impressively solid, strikers were undoubtedly suffering hardship. The savings of many had gone and debts were beginning to mount. Despite a Christmas sustained by the gifts and food parcels of well-wishers, incomes had dropped severely. Striking miners were receiving no strike pay, but at the end of November the government decided to 'deem' they were receiving an additional £1 per week from the union and subtract that £1 from the State benefits of their wives and children. Meanwhile, the area and national leadership of the union faced a large number of legal actions brought not, as expected at the beginning of the strike, by employers but by their own members. These actions were designed to get the strike declared unlawful and, having done this, to make the officials of the union personally liable for any further money spent on it. The union had not defended early actions and, judged to be in contempt of court, its funds had been sequestrated. Moved abroad before the strike began, these proved difficult to trace, and once found, hard to repatriate. The official receiver and the sequestrators were working to bring the NUM's £8·9 million funds back to the UK in early January 1985.

Whatever their ultimate outcomes, the campaigns of CND and the NUM are dramatic examples of a constant process. This chapter deals with the main types of pressure group and how they attempt to influence government policy.

Some leading pressure groups
In chapter 1 a distinction was made between *sectional* groups

Table 5.1 *The leading sectional groups in Britain*

Industry	Commerce	Finance	Professional	Trade Unions
Confederation of British Industry	Retail Consortium	The Bank of England	British Medical Association	Trades Union Congress
Smaller Businesses Association	Association of British Chambers of Commerce	Stock Exchange Council	British Dental Association	Amalgamated Union of Engineering Workers
British Institute of Management	National Chamber of Trade	City Liaison Committee	The Law Society	Electrical, Electronic, Telecommunications and Plumbing Union
Institute of Directors	Motor Agents Association	Committee of London Clearing Banks (e.g. National Westminster, Barclays, Midland, Lloyds)	Association of University Teachers	General, Municipal, and Boilermakers Union
Society of Motor Manufacturers and Traders	Road Haulage Association	Accepting Houses Committee (Merchant banks, e.g. Hambros)	Institute of Chartered Accountants	Transport and General Workers Union
Engineering Employers Federation	National Food and Drink Federation	Investment Protection Committee (Pension Funds)	Royal Institute of British Architects	National Union of Mineworkers
National Federation of Building Trades Employers	National Grocers Federation	The British Insurance Association (Joint stock insurance companies, e.g. Commercial Union Group)	Royal Institution of Chartered Surveyors	National Union of Railwaymen
United Kingdom Textile Manufacturers	National Federation of Wholesale Grocers and Provision Merchants	Building Societies Association	Institution of Mechanical Engineers	Union of Shop, Distributive and Allied Workers
British Footwear Manufacturers Federation	Cooperative Movement		Institution of Electrical Engineers	Association of Scientific, Technical and Managerial Staffs
National Association of Master Bakers, Confectioners and Caterers			Royal Town Planning Institute	National Union of Public Employees
National Farmers Union			Association of Metropolitan Authorities*	National and Local Government Officers' Association
			Association of County Councils*	National Union of Teachers
			District Councils Association*	
			London Boroughs Association*	

*Local Government Associations

Table 5.2 *The leading promotional groups in Britain*

Welfare	Environmental	Cultural	Recreational	Political	International
Shelter	National Trust	National Citizens Advice Bureau Council	National Playing Fields Association	Hansard Society	Amnesty International
Age Concern	Civic Trust	National Marriage Guidance Council	Ramblers Association	Electoral Reform Association	Anti-Apartheid Movement
Child Poverty Action Group	The Standing Committee on National Parks	Christian Union	Football Association	National Council for Civil Liberties	Oxfam
Disablement Income Group	Council for the Protection of Rural England	Students' Christian Movement	Marylebone Cricket Club	Campaign against Racial Discrimination	United Nations Association
Action for the Crippled Child	The Conservation Society	Mothers' Union	Youth Hostels Association	Consumers' Association	Parliamentary Group for World Government
Howard League for Penal Reform	Society for the Protection of Ancient Buildings	Lord's Day Observance Society	National Cyclists' Union	Aims of Industry	Rotary International
Abortion Law Reform Association	Automobile Association	National Federation Of Women's Institutes	Lawn Tennis Association	Economic League	English Speaking Union
Society for the Protection of the Unborn Child	Royal Automobile Club	National Viewers and Listeners Council	Amateur Athletics Association	Ratepayers' Associations	World Wildlife Fund UK
Action on Smoking and Health	Noise Abatement Society	British and Foreign Bible Society		Tenants' Associations	
Euthanasia Society	Association for Studies in the Conservation of Ancient Buildings	Royal Academy of Arts		Claimants' Unions	
Voluntary		British Humanist Association			
Family Planning Association	Friends of the Earth				
National Association for Mental Health	Royal Society for Nature Conservation				
Royal Society for the Prevention of Cruelty to Children	Woodland Trust				
Royal Society for the Prevention of Cruelty to Animals	Royal Society for the Protection of Birds				
	Farming and Wildlife Advisory Group				

based on occupation and *promotional* groups arising out of a shared cause or attitude. Tables 5.1 and 5.2 set out some leading groups within these categories. Promotional groups are so numerous that further subdivisions are often made. Thus the Child Poverty Action Group and Action for the Crippled Child are national organisations, whereas groups which campaign against the siting of motorways, airports and power stations generally mobilise local opinion. Further, organisations which support the poor or the handicapped are usually permanent whereas some campaigns like that of the campaign for lead free petrol (CLEAR) are formed on a temporary basis for a specific task. Of course, no categorisation is completely 'watertight'. Some groups have both sectional and promotional aspects. The Noise Abatement Society, for example, contains economically 'interested' manufacturers of equipment to suppress noise as well as members concerned simply to improve the environment. There is also an overlap between groups which speak for good causes, such as Shelter and Disablement Income Group, and 'purer' interest groups like trade unions, since they all seek to advance the material position of their clientèle. Nonetheless, the simple distinction remains important. Accordingly, the CBI and TUC (sectional) and Shelter and the Wing Airport Resistance Association (promotional) are used as examples of leading pressure groups in this opening section.

The Confederation of British Industry (CBI). The CBI is the main employers' organisation in Britain.[4] It was the product of a merger in 1965 between the British Employers' Confederation (1919), the Federation of British Industries (1916) and the National Association of British Manufacturers (1915). Its establishment was a consequence both of the need of modern government to consult with a broad organisation able to speak for the whole of industry and of the desire of industrialists for improved political representation. Indeed, many members value it less for any practical benefits they may derive than for its political role. In particular, the CBI can push governments into making concessions and generally act as a counterbalance to the influence of the trade unions. Its concerns, in dealings with government, range from the very general (e.g. prices and incomes policies) to extremely specific and technical matters such as dark smoke, mobile shops, polythene bags, chimney heights and pressure gauges. Its economic studies (on topics such as a wealth tax, gifts tax and investment incentives) and its prescriptions for the economy in publications, such as *The Road to Recovery* (1976), which called for reductions in taxation and in public expenditure, are attempts to influence 'informed opinion'. The CBI won concessions on prices policy, corporation tax and planning agreements from the 1974–1979 Labour Government, changed the emphasis in the 1975 Industry Act from job to profit creation and campaigned successfully to prevent legislation on the Bullock Report on industrial democracy in 1977.

The CBI has a membership of almost 11,000 companies and organisations, of which over 10,000 are industrial companies. It is still primarily a spokesman for manufacturing industry although some leading City institutions (the clearing banks, twenty merchant banks and ten large insurance companies) as well as the nationalised industries have become members. The retail sector has resisted absorption by the CBI and is separately organised in the Retail Consortium. The CBI has to represent the divergent interests of a membership which ranges from ICI to the family business. Despite its efforts, it has not always been successful and in 1971 many small firms withdrew to form the Society of Independent Manufacturers (later the Smaller Businesses Association).

The CBI has an annual budget of £2·6 million (1977) and a permanent UK staff of 440. Its General Council (400), which it sees as 'the parliament of industry', meets about eleven times in a year and is usually attended by between 150 and 200 members. In practice the Council is too large a body to serve as more than a sounding board for members' opinions and policy is made elsewhere. In particular, the Director-General is responsible for overall strategy and for particular emphases within the policy framework laid down by standing and special committees. The main standing committee is the General Purposes Committee, which is responsible for the handling of the CBI's relations with other organisations and for the use of resources. Thirty-four other standing committees deal with particular subjects such as wages and conditions, and economic, financial and employment policy. The Presidency of the CBI is an important post: in 1984, it was held by Sir James Cleminson, who succeeded Sir Campbell Fraser in May of that year. The Director-General has often had experience in government as well as in industry. Campbell Adamson, who held the post in the early 1970s, was formerly the government's chief industrial adviser, while John Methven, who become Director-General in 1976, had previously been with ICI for sixteen years and moved to the post from being Director-General of Fair Trading. Methven was succeeded in 1980 by Sir Terence Beckett, who was still Director-General in 1984.

Despite their efforts to keep in touch with members' opinions through twelve regional councils, Director-Generals find it difficult to reconcile the interests of small and large businesses, banks, insurance companies and nationalised industries. In 1971, internal strains arose when the heads of large companies argued for a severe reduction in the public sector while the Chairmen of the Nationalised Industries were simultaneously opposing the government's plan to sell parts of it back to private industry. Five years later, the Nationalised Industries formed their own pressure group within the organisation — the Group of Twenty-one. In general, CBI leaders have to strike a balance between cooperation with and resistance to the government of the day. They cannot hope to please all of their members all of the time, and what seems like a 'sell-out' to some will appear as narrow-minded obstructiveness to others.

These internal strains and problems of achieving a suitably 'balanced' response to government policy were evident again after 1979. Initially, as manufacturing industry suffered severely as a consequence of world recession and government pursuit of monetarist policy, the Director-General of the CBI called for a 'bare knuckle' fight with government. Clearly at that time, the CBI was giving priority to the needs of manufacturing industry against the interests of the banking, service and importing sectors which in general benefited from government policies. However, a sharp rejoinder by the Prime Minister forced the organisation to moderate its tone and during the 1983 general election it appeared to break away from its previous position of formal political neutrality by publicly endorsing the Conservative Party. The words of its president, Sir Campbell

Fraser, to Mrs Thatcher at its annual dinner to the effect that 'many of the people in this room will think that you deserve a second term of office' were criticised by leaders of the opposition parties. When the Chancellor reduced short interest and bank base rates by 0·5 per cent immediately after the election,·it was suggested that this was a 'reward' for the CBI's political support. A reduction in interest rates had been one of the measures of benefit to industry for which the CBI lobbied persistently after 1980. Others included the abolition of the National Insurance surcharge, a lowering of local authority rates on industrial and commercial premises and the reduction of energy, telecommunications, postal and water charges. All these measures, it was thought, if enacted, would lower costs and enable industry to be more competitive. In 1984, as well as urging the government to continue its cost-cutting and efficiency drive in the public sector by abolishing 460,000 (1 in 10) jobs in that sector, the CBI also called for the government to invest an extra £1 billion per year on roads, houses, bridges and sewers. These, it claimed, were falling into decay and, if improved, would greatly increase industrial competitiveness by reducing costs. In the previous five years, government spending on road building and improvements had declined by 60 per cent in real terms. 450,000 construction industry workers were unemployed. Relations between the CBI and government remained quite close. Indeed, many of the reforms which the government was seeking to promote – improvements in youth training and the encouragement of youth employment – depended on the cooperation of employers. Moreover, according to the CBI's own business prospects survey (May 1984), the economic revival was gaining pace. Although industrial redundancies were going to continue running at 5,000 per month, this compared with 40,000 per month at the depth of the recession. At its annual conference (November 1984), its Director-General could note that investment was 16 per cent up in 1983 and profits were recovering to the level of twenty years before.

The Trades Union Congress (TUC). The TUC was established in 1868 and is the main labour organisation in Britain. It contains over 100 affiliated unions with a combined membership of about

Table 5.3 *Trade union membership: the sixteen largest unions (1980)*

Transport and General Workers Union (TGWU)	2,073,000
Amalgamated Union of Engineering Workers (AUEW)	1,483,000
*General and Municipal Workers Union (GMWU)	965,000
National and Local Government Officers Association (NALGO)	729,000
National Union of Public Employees (NUPE)	712,000
Association of Scientific, Technical and Managerial Staffs (ASTMS)	471,000
Union of Shop, Distribution and Allied Trades (USDAW)	462,000
Electrical, Electronic, Telecommunications and Plumbing Union (EETPU)	420,000
Union of Construction, Allied Trades and Technicians (UCATT)	320,000
National Union of Teachers (NUT)	291,000
National Union of Mineworkers (NUM)	255,000
Civil and Public Servants Association (CPSA)	224,000
Confederation of Health Service Employees (COHSE)	215,000
Society of Graphical and Allied Trades (SOGAT)	203,000
Union of Post Office Workers (UPW)	197,000
National Union of Railwaymen (NUR)	180,000

*amalgamated 1982 with the Boilermakers Society to form the General, Municipal, Boilermakers and Allied Trades Union (GMBTU) with a membership of 960,000.

Source: 'Political Britain', *The Economist*, 1980, p. 24

11·5 million (1976). Most members are concentrated in a handful of big unions (Table 5.3). The vast majority of trade unionists belong to unions affiliated to the TUC, which can justly claim to represent the bulk of the unionised population. But only 44 per cent of workers belong to unions affiliated to it and the TUC cannot, therefore, claim to speak for the working population as a whole.

The political role of the TUC has increased greatly between 1945 and 1979 with the growth of government intervention in the economy, which has pushed the organisation into the formulation of views on a wide variety of social and economic policies. Like the CBI, the TUC not only collaborates with governments in these fields, it also acts as a critic. Since 1967 the TUC has published an *Economic Review* because it realised that very detailed analyses of the economic situation had to be offered if it were to influence the government.[5]

Despite its appearance of strength, the TUC is less powerful *within* the Labour movement than governments, and very often its General Secretary, would like it to be. Affiliated unions do not surrender their powers of independent action nor are the decisions of Congress binding on them. Expulsion is the ultimate sanction against member unions but is almost never used. The role of the TUC as conciliator in industrial disputes has become increasingly important and it participates in the Conciliation and Arbitration Service.

Overall responsibility for the formation of TUC policy lies with its annual Congress. However, considerable policy influence as well as formal executive powers, are held by the General Council (forty-eight members), which was elected after 1982 by a system ensuring the representation of small as well as large unions, and its General Secretary, an *ex officio* member of Council, who is assisted by a permanent staff and holds office for as long as Congress pleases. Norman Willis succeeded Len Murray in this post in 1984. The General Secretary requires considerable political skill in order to manage an organisation whose leading members frequently disagree with one another (for example, over the EEC and incomes policy) and who each control powerful unions of their own. Like large companies, big unions possess considerable independence from the 'umbrella' organisations to which they belong; they have a separate set of relationships with government and their leaders have considerable political authority in their own right.

Politically, the TUC aims to maintain or extend the legal freedoms of unions and to influence government economic policy. In 1969 and 1971 its refusal to cooperate thwarted the proposed industrial relations legislation of Labour and the actual legislation of the Conservatives. But it was unable to resist the Conservative Acts of 1980 (Prior), 1982 (Tebbit) and 1984 (Tebbit-King). The first two enactments limited lawful picketing to the pickets' own place of work. It became unfair to dismiss those with conscientious objections in a closed shop situation and financial compensation was provided for those who had been unfairly dismissed previously; new closed shops had to be approved by 80 per cent of the workers in a secret ballot; and employers were able to obtain injunctions against secondary picketing by workers not involved in the dispute. The Trade Union Act (1984) enabled union members to elect the governing body of their union by secret ballot at least once every five years; provided that trade unions should consult their members in a secret ballot before calling them out on strike (failure to do so meant they would forfeit any legal immunity to damages caused by the strike); and enacted that trade unionists should vote at least once every ten years on whether their union should continue to contribute money towards political activities. At the same time, the government won some fierce struggles against the unions, including the Iron and Steel Trades Confederation (1980) and the NUR (1982). In 1983, the print workers (National Graphical Association) and in 1984 the transport workers (TGWU) both ran foul of the new legislation. Nor, as we have seen, did matters look hopeful for the miners at the outset of 1985. The TUC countered with 'days of action' and threats to withdraw from economic institutions such as the National Economic Development Council (NEDC). Neither had had much effect by 1985, when TUC influence was at a low ebb.

Shelter. Shelter, the National Campaign for the Homeless, was founded in 1966. Its two major aims were to raise funds to house homeless people and to publicise the housing problem in order to raise the priority given to it by government. The launching of Shelter was helped by the almost simultaneous showing of the TV play dealing with homelessness, *Cathy Come Home*. Its first Director, Des Wilson, had a flair for publicity, using an astute combination of statistics and emotive rhetoric. One early slogan was 'Three million families in Britain will spend Christmas in slums' and Wilson invoked a sense of national crisis by calling for 'rescue operations'. These publicity campaigns captured the public imagination and have served as a model for other promotional groups concerned with the underprivileged. £500,000 was raised in Shelter's first month and by 1974 £3 million had been given to the housing associations which had helped to set it up.

Its income has fluctuated, although by 1976 Shelter was raising £50,000 annually. Its principal methods of persuasion and fund-raising have been media coverage, sponsored walks, and the distribution and sale of its own publications. Shelter also lobbies Ministers and local government officials and harries the political parties at their conferences. It set up an all-party parliamentary group in 1975.

Shelter has influenced legislation. The 1974 Housing Act made housing associations eligible for government grants to meet 10 per cent of their deficits, a step for which Shelter had long campaigned. The result of its successful lobby for greater security for tenants of furnished accommodation (achieved in the 1974 Rent Act) has been more controversial: some people argue that this had led to a reduction in rented accommodation but Shelter points out that this was in decline long before the Act and that, in any case, it has been offset by the growth of housing associations and housing aid centres. Shelter is still campaigning for legislation compelling local councils to house the homeless. It wants their present discretionary power turned into an obligation. Shelter, in fact, has become an important source of policy suggestions in the area of housing. It has consistently opposed the sale of council houses, criticised the tied cottage system and called for increased social control over the leading policies of building societies. It has condemned, in particular, building society policies which discriminate against properties that could be renovated in the inner cities. Policy has often been the subject of fierce debate within the association itself, with supporters divided on the relative priority to be given to short-term objectives (re-housing the homeless) as opposed to political campaigns which will produce results only in the longer term. Priority has usually been given to rehousing families in need: this absorbed two-thirds of Shelter's income in 1972–73.

Shelter was established on the basis of donations and local group activity, but in 1982 it launched a drive to attract a national membership of 10,000 on the basis of a subscription of £7·50 per annum. Its income of £900,000 in 1982 was mostly drawn from private donations. Its director, Neil McIntosh, said at this time that it was essential to awaken national awareness that the housing situation was deteriorating. By 1984, the organisation was predicting a major housing crisis in the late 1980s with families being split up or being forced to live in one room.

The Wing Airport Resistance Association (WARA). The Wing Airport Resistance Association is a classic example of a 'protest' pressure group of the 'I don't want it in my back garden or flying over my house' type. Its aim was to keep London's third airport away from Cublington, a small village in North Buckinghamshire, and it remains a celebrated incident in the long debate over the airport's siting. When the choice of Stansted was ruled out in 1968, the Roskill Commission was set up to consider the remaining alternatives. The four possible sites were Cublington, Thurleigh, Nuthampstead and Foulness. WARA was formed initially to give evidence before the Commission. It worked both locally, raising money and recruiting supporters, and nationally, where its London Committee, under the Chairman of the Association, concentrated on presenting the best possible case to Roskill. An experienced lawyer, Niall McDermott, was chosen to represent WARA before the Commission and sympathetic MPs were invited to become Vice-Presidents of the Association. 60,000 members were recruited in the first few months and the North Buckinghamshire area was flooded with publicity. The Association Secretary, John Pargeter, a local solicitor, organised the production of thousands of newsletters, information sheets, pamphlets and booklets. But Roskill, basing its conclusions on cost benefit analysis, still recommended Cublington as the site of the third airport.

WARA made it impossible for the government to carry out this proposal. A meeting of the London Committee was called within an hour of the news of Roskill's decision reaching the Chairman. The Committee launched a campaign both in parliament and in the media. WARA published its own criticism of the Roskill Report and disseminated it widely. It spent £3,500 on professional public relations advice. One successful publicity stunt held on two occasions involved hundreds of agricultural and industrial vehicles in a large procession through the threatened villages. The local campaign drew in thousands of outsiders to see for themselves the character of the places which would be destroyed. The established amenity movement supported the protesters. So did Professor Colin Buchanan, a dissenting member of the Roskill Commission, the Buckinghamshire County Council and many MPs. In the face of such a powerful campaign, the case against Foulness, which rested on the disturbance to wildlife, appeared very slight. On 26 April 1971 the Minister of Technology announced the decision to locate the third airport at Foulness. WARA had won.[6]

But, in fact, this was just one episode in a continuing saga. In the 1960s, prior to the WARA episode, the North West Essex and East Hertfordshire Preservation Association had fought a successful campaign to keep the third airport away from Stansted. For thirteen years after WARA's campaign to keep it out of Buckinghamshire, the question remained under discussion. Then came a second bombshell occurring just after the Hertfordshire and Essex protesters had celebrated the twentieth anniversary of their campaign, at the end of which (in 1965) the inspector had said it would be a calamity for the neighbourhood if a major airport were placed at Stansted. A 258-day inquiry conducted by a government-appointed inspector, Mr Graham Eyre, QC (published in November 1984), recommended the immediate development at Stansted of a single-runway airport capable of handling 15 million passengers a year, rising to 25 million. When the Roskill Commission considered 100 sites for a new London airport, Stansted, as has been seen, was not even on the shortlist. It had been put back at the top of the government's shortlist in 1979, when local protesters raised quarter of a million pounds to fight it. Now they must do so again. This time, however, they had some powerful allies. Airports in the Midlands and North were anxious to obtain the development and, by mid-December, 225 MPs of all parties including many Conservatives had signed a motion calling for the airport to be build in the north.

Patterns of pressure

Pressure group tactics can vary a great deal. They may vary according to the nature of the group, its cause, the degree of political acceptance it has attained and the amount of actual and potential support which it can command. The character of the political system also affects strategy. For, if they are to succeed, pressure groups must clearly understand how power is distributed in society.

It used to be said that pressure groups in Britain aimed at the executive. Because local authorities lacked real independence and because the government had tight control of the House of Commons, it made sense for groups to concentrate on Ministers and civil servants. Although there is still much truth in this view, pressure group activity can no longer be said to conform to a single pattern. Campaigns in the 1970s and 1980s, such as Shelter and CND have been directed less at Cabinets and Ministries than at a combination of informed and popular opinion, the media, parliament and local government, on the one hand, and the wider public on the other. But it would not necessarily be correct to conclude from this that sectional groups go for Whitehall while promotional groups run broader campaigns, nor is it true that sectional groups tackle the ministries, parliament and the public in successive stages, while promotional groups reverse the process. Many groups seek influence at all levels *simultaneously*.[7] This section describes the pattern of relationships which has arisen between the pressure groups and the ministries, parliament and public opinion.

Pressure groups and government. Sectional groups are linked with politicians and civil servants by a well established system of formal and informal contacts. Formal contacts take place on Royal Commissions, Committees of Inquiry and Departmental Advisory Committees. For example, both the TUC and CBI were represented on the Royal Commission on the Reform of the Trade Unions and Employers' Associations (1965–68). Contacts are frequent. There have been over one thousand tribunals of inquiry this century and there were twenty-nine Royal Commissions between 1945 and 1974. Many of these deal with issues of concern to management and unions. *Ad hoc* departmental advisory committees also provide contacts. The Houghton Committee on the Pay of Non-University Teachers (1974–75) included representatives of both teacher unions and local authority associations. At the highest level, there is a set of economic institutions of which the most prominent is the National Economic Development Council. This was established in 1961 to provide up-to-date economic advice and analysis. There are also public boards such as the Price Commission and the Monopolies Commission. Such institutions constitute the top of the pyramid of formal links. Most contacts occur lower down the Whitehall sectional group hierarchy in meetings between civil servants and pressure group spokesmen on departmental standing advisory committees. In 1974 producer groups were represented on about five hundred of these and the TUC alone was present on forty.

Much of the business between pressure groups and public officials is done in an informal, 'unofficial' way by letter, telephone and face-to-face discussion. These informal contacts may prepare the way for a later formal meeting by discovering and resolving possible difficulties in advance, or they may be used to sound out the views of a department or group on proposed legislation, and so on. What matters is that both formal and informal consultations are part of the routine processes of British government; links are close, continuous and generally amicable. Sometimes consultation with affected groups is required by statute; under the 1947 Agriculture Act, for example, the Minister of Agriculture has to consult with spokesmen for the farmers; more often, it is simply considered to be a duty both by governments and by the groups themselves. Pressure groups regard a lack of consultation as a criticism of the government and sometimes, even, as a good reason for not complying with resultant legislation. The trade union movement adopted this latter attitude towards the Industrial Relations Act 1971.

Of course, not all pressure groups are recognised by government as having the right to be consulted; not all are *legitimised*. This distinction, between groups which have an accepted right to be consulted by government and those which do not, is important. In education, the teachers' unions and the local authorities are legitimised groups; the Society of Teachers opposed to Physical Punishment and the Comprehensive Schools Association are not. Very few of the groups which campaign on environmental issues are automatically consulted about them. Of course, the line between legitimised and non-legitimised status can be crossed; the National Association of Schoolmasters, for example, waged a strong and successful campaign for the right to be represented on the Burnham Committee which negotiates teachers' salaries. In deciding whether to legitimise a group, a government has to consider its representativeness within its field and also to weigh the cases of rival groups claiming to speak for the same interests. In return for recognition, governments require restraint and moderation on the part of a group. It must know how to keep quiet about the substance of consultations and it must refrain from criticism of Ministers and officials. The behaviour of the National Union of Students, a legitimised group which maintains an aggressive and critical stance, is a rare exception to this convention.[8]

Both sides gain from this system of group representation. Pressure groups get valuable advance information about governments' intentions and the chance to influence their policies. The benefits derived by governments may be less obvious at first sight. In fact, there are three: advice and information; acquiescence in, or even assent to, their proposals; and, quite often, assistance with the administration of policies.

Governments may ask for the recommendations of a group within a particular policy field or for likely reactions to a particular proposal. Consultation enables a government to anticipate weaknesses and objections; even if it is subsequently unable to remedy these, at least it will be able to have its reply ready. Government thereby gains in authority as the likelihood of losing face is diminished. Departments have a general need to keep up-to-date with events in their field. But often they have more specific reasons for seeking information from groups: a question may have been asked in parliament and the Minister will have to be briefed for his reply; specialised, technical information may also be needed in the drafting of legislation.

Group acquiescence is important to government because British political culture places a high value on compromise and the avoidance of overt dissension. The desire of governments to win agreement can slow down the decision-making process. Thus legislation against vehicle noise and proposals for the compulsory fitting of seat belts were seriously delayed because the Ministry of Transport was reluctant to impose them on the motor industry against the objections of its spokesman, the Society of Motor Manufacturers and Traders; to have done so would have disrupted a relationship in which much is normally achieved by private agreement.[9]

Governments often require not only information and consent from pressure groups but also actual help in the administration of policies. The Law Society, for example, administers the legal aid scheme. In the mid-1970s, the TUC and the CBI were involved in the administration of the Manpower Services Commission (1974), which is responsible for job creation, job placement and training; the Health and Safety Commission (1975), which deals with health and safety at work; and the Conciliation and Arbitration Council (1976), which is concerned with industrial conciliation. The TUC and CBI each nominate three members to these bodies.

Pressure groups and parliament. Parliament is generally a less important focus of group pressure than Whitehall, but it is not neglected either. Not all legislation reaching the House is beyond amendment, and a group acting through a sympathetic MP may be able to persuade a Minister to 'think again' on some aspect of a Bill. On major government legislation, of course, substantial changes are unlikely, but concessions on points of detail may still be won at the committee stage. Groups may at least force Ministers to clarify ambiguous points or gain assurances (favourable to themselves) on the interpretation of particular clauses. Where a free vote is allowed, as with the conscience legislation of the 1960s, they may hope to wield far more influence. Groups which aim to change the law need parliamentary sponsors for their Bills; thus Sidney Silverman sponsored the legislation to abolish capital punishment, and David Steel proposed the measure which liberalised the abortion law. Furthermore, in the absence of the Party Whips, opposing groups can vie for the voting support of MPs. More generally, since parliament retains considerable status as a forum of debate, groups may seek influence by means of Parliamentary Questions. Often they will be fobbed off, but at least they will gain useful publicity and may even prompt further inquiry into the cause they are promoting.

Groups establish parliamentary connections in a number of ways. Some, like local authority and trade associations, offer MPs honorary positions as directors or advisers. Others try to recruit them to their executives. Groups such as the Association of British Chambers of Commerce and the RSPCA make one of their officials specifically responsible for maintaining contacts with MPs. These officials lobby MPs, organise meetings and contact relevant party groups. Through sympathetic MPs they may also sponsor questions in the House, provide information with which to counter questions hostile to their interests, move amendments, table substantive motions and put forward proposals in Private Members' Bills. Pressure groups often receive sympathetic support from MPs which cuts across party lines: on conscience issues, for instance, or on regional economic policy. Thus, all Lancashire MPs will share a concern with textile manufacturers about prospects for the textile industry.

The most direct link between an interest group and parliament lies in the sponsorship of MPs by trade unions. At the 1983 general election, trade unions sponsored 154 Labour candidates of whom 115 were elected (see Table 5.4 for the numbers sponsored by individual unions). Since 1945 important changes have taken place in the composition of the trade union group of MPs. The NUM and NUR sponsor fewer MPs as their memberships have declined, but this is offset by increased sponsorship from others such as the AUEW and from new white-collar unions such as NUPE and ASTMS. In some cases, the kind of candidate sponsored has also changed. The GMWU, for example, has increasingly adopted graduates with middle class professional backgrounds rather than rank-and-file union officials. But the proportion of trade union MPs in the PLP has remained roughly constant since 1945; it even increased slightly in the 1970s. Sponsored MPs receive help with election and parliamentary expenses and often also small annual payments. Sponsorship perhaps brings 'symbolic' gain – an increased working-class presence in the House of Commons – rather than direct benefits. Trade unions may not instruct their MPs how to speak or vote in parliament since this would constitute a breach of parliamentary privilege.[10]

Business, commercial and financial interests are also well represented in parliament, although not by direct sponsorship. Over half of all MPs, including a majority of Conservatives and a minority of Labour members, have some links with business and

Table 5.4 *Candidates sponsored by trade unions in 1983*

	Total	Elected
Transport and General Workers' Union	30	25
Amalgamated Union of Engineering Workers	27	17
National Union of Mineworkers	14	14
General, Municipal, Boilermakers and Allied Trades Union	14	11
Association of Scientific, Technical and Managerial Staffs	11	10
National Union of Railwaymen	12	10
National Union of Public Employees	10	4
Association of Professional, Executive, Clerical and Computer Staff	3	3
Confederation of Health Service Employees	3	3
Electrical, Electronic, Telecommunications & Plumbing Trades Union	7	3
Post Office Engineering Union	3	3
Society of Graphical and Allied Trades '82	2	2
Union of Shop, Distributive and Allied Workers	2	2
Iron & Steel Trades Confederation	3	1
Union of Construction, Allied Trades and Technicians	2	1
Society of Lithographic Artists Designers Engravers and Process Workers	2	1
7 other Unions all with 1 candidate, 5 of whom were elected, and ASLEF with 2 candidates neither of whom were elected	9	5
Total union-sponsored	154	115

Source: D. Butler and D. Kavanagh, *The British General Election of 1983*, Macmillan, p. 240

commerce. MPs are executives, consultants and major share-holders as well as chairmen, directors and partners of business concerns. Business connections are so widespread that James Callaghan remarked in 1965: 'When I look at some Members discussing the Finance Bill I do not think of them as the Hon. Member for X, Y or Z. I look at them and say 'investment trusts', 'capital speculators' or 'that is the fellow who is the Stock Exchange man who makes a profit on gilt-edged'.[11] The need for MPs to have these outside financial interests is usually related to the relatively low pay of MPs compared with other people of similar education, ability and experience.

It is hard to say how far these interests and links with outside organisations actually affect MPs' behaviour. Most academic writers have concluded that their influence is rather slight; for example, a study of union-sponsored MPs during the defence dispute of 1960–61 and the discussion of incomes policy, 1966–70, has argued that 'they responded to the demands of the Party Whips rather than the policy positions of their own unions';[12] on the other hand, many sponsored MPs were among Labour opponents of the Industrial Relations Bill in 1969. Some unions, moreover, have pressed for special causes through their sponsored MPs; the ASTMS lobby in 1965 for legislation to force all employers to give redundancy pay is an example.

During the 1970s, controversy about the influence of outside interests grew. In 1975, after concern had been expressed about the relations between MPs and public relations firms, parliament decided to institute and publish a register of interests. This would be revised three or four times a year, and MPs would disclose in it the sources (but not the amount) of their personal incomes and other interests. But the obligation to disclose an interest is imposed only by resolution of the House, not by legislation. Hence MPs who refuse to do so, as Enoch Powell did, commit only a contempt of parliament and not a breach of the law.[13]

It is, of course, customary for MPs to declare their interest at the beginning of any debate to which they contribute. However, a Commons Select Committee of Inquiry which in 1977 reported on dealings between certain MPs and the architect, John Poulson, who was imprisoned for corruption in 1974, gave reason to doubt whether full declarations of interest were always made.

It criticised three MPs for 'conduct inconsistent with the standards which the House is entitled to expect from its members'. Poulson paid considerable sums of money to MPs to advance his interests. Had a compulsory register of interests existed at the time the dealings took place, these MPs, who were accused of failing to reveal their interests rather than possessing them, would probably not have come under criticism.

The relationship between groups and their parliamentary spokesmen is not contractual and MPs who choose to represent outside interests can normally sever such links if they wish. A distinction should also be made between advocacy of a cause for a fee or retainer and the advancement of an argument by a Member who 'through a continuing association with an industry, service or concern from which he may draw some remuneration, is able to draw upon specialist knowledge of the subject under debate'.[14] Generally, it seems that the possession of outside interests by MPs has normally been considered acceptable so long as two conditions are fulfilled: these are that the interests are declared openly and that the outside interest does not try to dictate directly to an MP on how he speaks and votes.

Members of Parliament have to register their paid directorships, paid employments, paying clients, major stakes in companies and other parliamentary perquisites such as sponsored overseas trips. Often, however, these declarations are so vague that it is impossible to gauge the extent of the interest. According to the political editor of *The Observer*, the usual payment to MPs in 1984 for serving as parliamentary consultants for business companies (e.g. drugs, tobacco) was between £10,000–£20,000. Fees for one-off services are smaller. For example, MPs might receive £200 from an outside interest for putting down a written question, and 'considerably more' for asking oral questions. At present, some lobbyists directly fund all-party House of Commons committees, use accommodating MPs to book private House of Commons rooms to impress their clients and attach their employees to MPs as 'research assistants'. By this last-named device, they gain preferential access to White Papers and House of Commons documents as well as to Ministers and other MPs. One way of improving this situation might be to require MPs to declare the precise amount of the fees they receive from lobbyists as well as listing the full range of clients for whom they act. Another suggestion is for lobbyists themselves to register and to file quarterly returns of all the payments they make, as they have to do in the United States.

Present arrangements may be an insufficient safeguard of the public interest. Take, for instance, the Commons debate on the Cable bill in 1984. Huge commercial interests were at stake. During its committee proceedings, half the Conservative backbenchers declared that they had either a direct or an indirect financial interest. One MP told the Committee that he had a 75 per cent share in one of the eleven pilot cable franchises, and later also said that he was acting as an adviser to a company with a financial stake in Capitol Radio.[15] Political commentators are becoming concerned at the sheer extent of the financial stake of legislators in the matters on which they legislate. A genuine issue of their impartiality has been raised.

Public campaigns. One vital form of pressure is the public campaign. These fall into two broad categories. First, there are long-term educational and propaganda campaigns to produce significant shifts of public opinion. An example would be the work of Shelter to alert people to the problems of homelessness, or the lobby to increase aid to the underdeveloped countries. Second, there are short campaigns designed to mobilise public opinion against a specific threat and, if possible, to avert it. Protest and environmental campaigns like that of WARA are of this type; so are those often waged by industrial groups, industries and firms against nationalisation. The appearance of books with titles such as *How to Run a Pressure Group* indicates the growing political significance of these public campaigns.[16]

The way in which a group allocates effort between such targets as the civil service, parliament, the media and the public depends on both the nature of the group and its cause. Protest groups such as WARA have no alternative but to seek maximum publicity: large-scale public support is their only hope of success.

In the 1970s environmentalist groups ran successful campaigns which depended upon wide publicity. The Conservation Society publicised information about illicit dumping of cyanide wastes in 1971. The government had had proposals from an official committee for the control of toxic wastes for two years, but, after the publicisation of the issue rushed a Bill through parliament to control it within three months. In 1978, the Greenpeace vessel *Rainbow Warrior* interrupted a proposed seal cull on Orkney and received heavy media coverage. This led the Secretary of State for Scotland, who had ordered the cull, to call it off. But some promotional groups run the risk of disrupting a well-established relationship with Whitehall if they 'go public'. For this reason, the Howard League for Penal Reform was unwilling to organise a public campaign for the abolition of capital punishment; this was done by a specially created organisation, the National Campaign for the Abolition of Capital Punishment. Even this campaign turned to mass publicity only reluctantly, when it had failed to persuade the Home Office and party leaderships.

Indeed, on controversial issues, mass publicity may be counter-productive. Most people's minds are already made up and a short campaign is as likely to foment hostile reactions as to change minds. Such campaigns may also encourage the formation of organisations to present the opposite point of view and the effectiveness of any publicity with inevitably be reduced both by the appearance of adverse propaganda and by the sheer proliferation of groups in the field. Many groups, therefore, aim at *informed* rather than mass opinion. This was the strategy of the Abortion Law Reform Association and the Homosexual Law Reform Society in the 1960s.[17] Of course, informed and mass opinion are not mutually exclusive targets: often, groups will lobby on several fronts simultaneously. The National Parks Campaign and the British Roads Federation both pursue public campaigns while also maintaining official contacts with Whitehall. Clearly, no single generalisation can cover every example of pressure group activity.

Resources. A successful campaign depends on resources as well as a sound strategy. Political resources include leadership, money, a group's case and the size and quality of its membership. Leadership is vital and styles of leadership vary greatly ranging from the blunt and forceful methods of powerful trade union leaders to the suave self-confidence of someone like Frank Field (formerly of Child Poverty Action, Labour MP for Birkenhead since May 1979). A style appropriate to the worlds of business or trade unionism would not necessarily work elsewhere. Moreover, the brand of leadership suited to a protest or promotional group differs from the more responsible style demanded of the leader of a legitimised managerial group, such as the Association of Education Committees. Such leaders, often engaged in delicate negotiations, generally shun publicity which might compromise their position or that of the government and consequently might jeopardise the outcome of their talks.

Good leaders can rarely convert a weak case into a strong one but they can at least make the most of it. The quality of argument *matters*. An ability to manipulate statistics can be useful. Frank Field strengthened the case for bigger family allowances by pointing out that they have been increased far less often since 1948 than payments such as pensions, and unemployment, sickness and supplementary benefits.[18] The CPAG's campaign helped to raise child benefit from £2·35 in 1978 to £4·75 in November 1980. Similarly, WARA's campaign against the findings of the Roskill Commission required a complex, technical evaluation of its use of cost-benefit analysis. Sometimes, it strengthens a group's position, especially in environmental protests, to be able to produce a viable alternative scheme. The weakness of objections to Manchester Corporation's plan to extract water from Ullswater and Windermere was their failure not only to show that Manchester had exaggerated its need for water but also to suggest a practicable alternative.[19]

The possession and expenditure of large sums of money does not inevitably bring political success. The very costly anti-nationalisation campaigns run by business since 1945 have often failed. Nevertheless, it is still an important political resource, and one in which promotional groups are generally much worse off than their sectional counterparts. Shelter's ability to raise about £500,000 per annum, Friends of the Earth's ability to spend £50,000 on the Windscale inquiry (1977) and WARA's collection of £44,000 to pay for evidence to the Roskill commission (1969–70) are conspicuous successes. Most promotional groups, however, have to subsist on small incomes. Throughout the 1950s and early 1960s, for example, the Abortion Law Reform Association spend between £50 and £600 per year. Its income rose to £6,000 in 1967, but this was quite exceptional; the minute income of its earlier years is more typical of the small radical or protest group than its relative affluence later.[20] Lack of resources can be a considerable handicap to protest groups. At the Sizewell inquiry, for example, environmentalist protestors required considerable resources in order to be able to cope with the quantity and technicality of the information in a situation in which their opponent, the Central Electricity Generating Board, could call upon massive funds and expertise.

The size of a group's membership obviously matters. People speak of the 'big battalions' like the CBI and TUC and it is largely correct that the leader of the TGWU is a powerful figure because he represents 1·75 million workers. But sheer size is not the only significant factor; it can be offset by other characteristics which may be called *density* and *representativeness*. The notion of *primary density* in regard to groups draws attention to their member–potential member ratio. Of all those eligible for membership of a given organisation, it refers to the percentage who actually are members; for example, the proportion of the workforce which belongs to trade unions, of industrial firms which have joined the CBI, of miners in the National Union of Mineworkers.[21] Clearly, an organisation can be very large and yet still be vulnerable to the charge that it does not speak for a very large proportion of its potential membership. The Conservative Party, for example, has often pointed out that, while, in absolute terms, the British trade union movement is very large (11·6 million), in fact it represents only 48 per cent of all employees.[22] To the extent that people are influenced by such arguments, the political influence of the trade union movement is effectively diminished.

Promotional groups tend to have smaller memberships than sectional groups. But, unlike groups whose prospective membership is in an important sense 'given' by their performing a particular occupation, they have to attract their memberships from scratch. The ability of groups like WARA (60,000), CND (110,000) and the National Campaign for the Abolition of Capital Punishment (30,000) to gain such huge followings represents a very considerable achievement. More usually, membership is numbered in a few thousands (for example, the Homosexual Law

Reform Society had 2,000 members) or even in hundreds; 5,000 is a good membership for a cause group and 10,000 is exceptional.[23]

Again, size is not everything. Thus, the apparent disadvantage in size possessed by the Abortion Law Reform Association (1,000 members in 1966) was counteracted in two ways: the main cause group opposing it, the Society for the Protection of the Unborn Child, was even smaller (about one-third the size) and the much larger organisations, the Catholic Church and medical associations, which also opposed it, were 'partial' groups which were sometimes slow to organise. Membership size is not necessarily even a very reliable measure of public support. ALRA, for example, benefited from a series of opinion polls which suggested that a majority of the public, of women and of doctors supported legalised abortion in certain circumstances. Polls in 1968 also showed a majority in favour of easier divorce. This is not to suggest that public support is always necessary to the success of a group. Majority opinion opposed both homosexual law reform and the abolition of capital punishment.[24] It is simply to say that a promotional group almost always enjoys public support far beyond its limited membership.

The idea of density hardly applies to promotional groups since they lack a clearly identifiable potential membership. For example, ALRA included as members only a tiny percentage (0.2 per cent) of the women who were estimated to have had illegal abortions between 1945 and 1965. Its political persuasiveness derived from the quality of its membership, which consisted predominantly of young and middle-aged, well-educated, middle-class women.[25]

The second factor which may reduce the impact of sheer size is representativeness. How far do pressure group spokesmen literally represent the views of their members? The question may be asked about any kind of group which seeks political influence, whether sectional or promotional, interest or cause. The general point here is that any group which seeks political influence will be weakened if its leadership is out of touch with the rank-and-file or if its membership is apathetic or divided; the secession of the Smaller Businesses Association from the CBI illustrates the danger of schisms.

6 Parties and Pressure Groups: Trends and Problems

The contemporary political system

The last three chapters have presented a detailed description of the parties and pressure groups which form major elements in the British political system. The final two chapters examine their impact on the system as a whole. In particular, the working of the system is discussed in terms of such criteria as effectiveness, fairness, choice and participation. This chapter begins with a consideration of recent trends in party and pressure group behaviour and then goes on to examine some leading contemporary interpretations of their influence on political life.

A quarter of a century ago the two-party system was in its heyday. The two major parties between them regularly polled over 90 per cent of the total vote and the fact that the victorious party normally polled just under 50 per cent of the vote was widely seen as entitling it to take decisions in the national interest. There was broad agreement between the parties to administer a mixed enterprise welfare state with at most only modest changes and with priority given to keeping employment at a high level. It was the age of 'consensus' politics. The similarities between the parties were widely regarded as of greater political significance than their differences. Voters were thought to be generally well satisfied with the amount of say and choice given them under this system, since minor parties received few votes and promotional pressure groups were of little account in political life.[1] British parliamentary democracy was commonly regarded as providing stable, effective government.

This description is only partly true now. As earlier chapters have shown, the major parties still alternate in government. But together they poll a much smaller proportion of the total vote – 75 per cent in the two 1974 elections, up to 80 per cent in 1979 but down to only 70 per cent in 1983. Moreover, the winning party in the last two elections has gained little over two-fifths of the total vote and in the previous two gained under two-fifths of the total vote. The steady growth in support for minor parties throughout the 1970s and early 1980s completed the discomfiture of Labour and the Conservatives. Whereas in 1959, minor parties got seven seats and 6·8 per cent of the total vote, in 1983 they won forty-four seats and gained 30 per cent of the total vote. Over 25 per cent of voters chose the Alliance. Of course, the rise of the minor parties should not be exaggerated. The 'first past the post' electoral system protected the major parties against the consequences of their declining popularity and enabled their parliamentary domination to continue. Thus, 8·2 million Alliance and nationalist votes brought a mere twenty-seven parliamentary seats; but 8·5 million Labour votes were worth 209 seats; and 13 million Conservative votes gained that party a massive 397 seats. The Conservatives received 4·8 million votes fewer than their political opponents on the British mainland but won 161 more seats. So large was the Conservative majority that the minor parties did not even enjoy that bargaining relationship with government which they had briefly held between 1974 and 1979. Critics made two points. First, the composition of the House of Commons fell a long way short of representing the wishes of the electorate. Alliance voters could feel especially aggrieved because whereas it took 32,777 votes to elect a Conservative MP and 40,482 votes to return a Labour MP, it required 338,089 votes to send an Alliance representative to the House of Commons. Second, despite its huge parliamentary majority, the Conservative Party represented only a minority of voters. At worst, this impaired its claims to speak for the nation but at best it suggested that the party ought to proceed cautiously and take care not to press mere party interests too hard.

If government more obviously represented a minority of the electorate (*despite* its vast majority in parliament), it was also more extreme government than it had been a quarter of a century previously. In the 1970s, differences between the parties became more clearly defined. The broad consensus on social and economic policy which prevailed in the 1950s was displaced from the centre of the political arena by the parties' disagreements on new issues such as economic growth, the control of inflation and relations with the European Community. Governments were forced to adopt incomes policies and to attempt to reform industrial relations. In all these fields, the major parties attempted to reverse each other's policies. The Conservatives rejected Labour's incomes policy in 1970 and abolished the Prices and Incomes Board. After February 1974 the Labour Party repealed the Heath government's Industrial Relations Act and subsequently replaced the Conservatives' statutory incomes policy with a voluntary one.

Furthermore, the two parties also made frequent 'U-turns' in their own policies and reneged on election promises. The Labour Party applied to join the Common Market in power and then came close to opposing the step out of office; in government, it favoured a statutory incomes policy and attempted to provide a legal framework for collective bargaining; in opposition, it came out against both policies. The Conservatives were elected in 1970 on a pledge to reduce public expenditure and government support for ailing industries; within two years, the party had adopted a statutory incomes policy and rescued Rolls-Royce and Upper Clyde Shipbuilders with public funds; during their term of office, the ratio of public expenditure to Gross National Product continued to rise.

Of course, reversals of policy may sometimes be justified as necessary and flexible responses to changed circumstances. But by the late 1970s this did not seem to be the case. A wide range of policies had been tried to promote economic growth, to bring inflation under control and to improve industrial relations, with only a small degree of success. It may be that the policies of the two main parties succeeded as well as could reasonably have been expected; but to the electorate both had persistently failed to achieve the policy objectives which they themselves identified as essential to the national interest and to their own continuation in office.

The conclusion seemed inescapable that the effectiveness of governments was diminishing. Not only were they apparently incapable of carrying out important goals they set for themselves, even when they did so their policies were subject to swift reversal when they lost power. Nor was this all. Governments in the 1970s also came under increasing pressure from powerful outside interests. In order to succeed, governments needed more than a majority in the House of Commons; they had to carry the country with them. To do this, they generally had to win the support of the big sectional interest groups. Genuine success required the achievement of policy goals, and pressure groups were able to influence the political effectiveness of governments far more than in the 1950s. Their influence on policy-making is the third important characteristic distinguishing the political system of the 1970s from that of the 1950s.

In 1969 trade union opposition forced the Labour Cabinet to abandon its Industrial Relations Bill and destroyed its incomes policy. When the Conservative Government introduced its industrial relations legislation, the main principles of which, it made clear, were non-negotiable, the unions launched an even greater onslaught: by the end of 1973, non-cooperation had rendered large sections of the Act unworkable. The unions showed the impotence of government to enforce legislation on a well-organised section of the community which was determined to resist it. In June 1974 a political strike by the Ulster Workers' Council brought down the Coalition Government at Stormont led by Brian Faulkner. Nor was it only the trade unions which demonstrated their power over government policies. Industrialists consistently resisted the exhortations of governments to raise levels of investment, and early in 1977 the CBI indicated its opposition to the idea of worker directors elected solely through the trade unions (as proposed by the Bullock Commission): whatever system of worker participation the government devised would have to receive the assent of the leading business organisation.

In the mid-1970s it was often said that the trade unions, rather than parliament or the elected government, 'ran the country'. This was partly a result of the February 1974 general election at which the Conservative Party asked the electorate for support in resisting the miners' demands: the Conservatives lost their parliamentary majority and were unable to continue in office; and the miners gained a pay rise of over 30 per cent. Although they won four more seats than the Conservatives, the Labour Party did not gain an overall majority either. Nevertheless, the general conclusion drawn by many commentators was that the Conservatives had 'lost' and that the miners had 'won'.

The first two years of the subsequent Labour Governments suggested more decisively that power had passed to the interest groups, in particular to the TUC. In opposition after 1970, Labour had resolved not to allow the Party and the unions to drift apart as they had done between 1966 and 1970. The proposals of the TUC-Labour Party Liaison Committee formed the basis of both Labour's manifestoes in 1974 and of its policies during its first two years of office. This arrangement between the party and the unions was usually referred to as the 'Social Contract'. In return for promises of wage restraint, the party promised to repeal much Conservative legislation and to implement a costly and wide-ranging programme of social policies. Thus the Labour Government repealed the Conservatives' Industrial Relations and Housing Finance Acts, introduced an immediate pensions increase and a reform of the system of state pensions as well as increased subsidies to council tenants and security of tenure to tenants in private furnished accommodation; it also nationalised the aircraft and shipbuilding industries and development land, increased tax rates on higher incomes and (by the Employment Protection Act) gave new rights to workers and trade unions. All these measures, and many more, were directly inspired by the TUC. Yet large wage settlements continued and inflation remained at a higher rate than in most of the industrialised world. In the first half of 1975, wage settlements averaged 39·7 per cent in the public sector and 33 per cent in the private sector.[2]

Parties, therefore, not only bargained with the great producer groups, they often got the worst of the bargains struck. The rise of promotional groups completed their discomfiture. The new cause groups, such as Shelter, the CPAG and the Disablement Income Group, also staked a major claim in the initiation of policy; at the same time, protest groups such as WARA joined with sectional groups in opposing various aspects of government programmes. Government policies in housing, social welfare and the environment after the mid-1960s all reflect the impact of these groups. The proliferation of voluntary organisation indicated that many social needs were not being met by the public authorities and the two major political parties.[3]

So far it has been contended that three features distinguish the political system of party and pressure group representation which emerged in the 1970s from its predecessor in the 1950s. First, the virtual two-party monopoly has been eroded by the formation of, and growth in support for, the Liberals, the SDP and the nationalist parties. Their emergence has increased voter choice but also voter frustration because the party composition of parliament has not reflected the often large degree of electoral success achieved by the minor parties. Second, parties have taken up more extreme and contrasting positions, party disagreement has intensified and this has affected considerably the workings of British government. Consensus has evaporated and government has been punctuated by 'U-turns' (when a party goes back on its own manifesto promises) and about-turns (when it reverses its predecessor's policies). Third, in order to carry out its policies, the governing party requires the cooperation of the major sectional groups. So that a wider range of social needs can be met, campaigning groups have formed and now complement the activities of parties. The overall effect of these changes has been to reduce both the authority and the effectiveness of government.

To what extent have these three trends continued under Conservative Governments after 1979? In part, the answer has already been given to the first point. Despite their huge House of Commons majority, the Conservatives can by no means be said to have received an enthusiastic popular mandate in 1983. Even with the help of the 'Falklands factor', their overall percentage of the total vote was slightly lower than in 1979. In a sense, they triumphed by default, winning as a result of Labour's shortcomings and the division of the opposition vote between Labour and the Alliance. Labour for their part did very badly indeed, obtaining their lowest share of the popular vote since 1918. The 1983 election confirmed and intensified, therefore, both the diminishing support for the two major parties and the accompanying trend towards an *electoral* multi-partyism which was barely reflected in the House of Commons. Conservative backbench rebellions continued in the new parliament and constituted the most effective, although inadequate, check on the Government's activities.

With reference to the second theme, the two major parties have seldom if ever been further apart than they were in 1983. Labour had veered strongly towards the left in opposition and went to the electorate on a 'Socialist' programme. Meanwhile, the Conservatives had continued their rightward shift under the leadership of Mrs Thatcher. This left the centre ground to be occupied by the Alliance, which it did by offering 'moderate' consensus government and attacking both the major parties as 'under the thumb' of the big sectional interests. In effect, the Conservatives sought a mandate to continue the national change of direction they began after 1979. Although the success of the change of direction they carried out in their first administration is a matter of controversy, there is no doubt that an 'about-turn' took place. The Labour Government under James Callaghan (1976–1979) began the policy of monetarism which gave the control of inflation priority over the achievement of full employment or a faster rate of growth as objectives of economic policy. But it did so without ever becoming committed to 'monetarism' as a doctrine. Moreover, it continued in concert with the trade union movement to operate a non-statutory incomes policy across both the private and the public sector. This policy collapsed in 1979 in a wave of strikes involving tanker drivers, water workers, ambulance drivers, sewerage workers and dustmen – the so-called 'winter of discontent'.[4] By contrast, Mrs Thatcher's first Conservative Government (1979–1983) implemented a doctrinaire monetarism, abandoning controls on pay, prices and dividends. Whilst setting a flexible yet covert guideline for public sector wages by means of cash limits, it permitted private sector wages to be determined by free collective bargaining. There were sharp changes in other policy areas, too. The Labour Government sought further nationalisation, the progressive withdrawal of private medicine from NHS hospitals and the ending of selection in secondary education. The Conservative Government carried out a radical policy of privatisation. By 1983, it had sold off to the private sector half its shares in British Aerospace, nearly half its shares in Cable and Wireless, British Rail's hovercraft and hotels and the National Enterprise Board's interests in

Ferranti, ICL, Fairey and other groups. It had sold off completely the National Freight Corporation, Amersham International (a
radio-chemical firm), Associated British Ports, the British Leyland offshoots Alvis, Prestcold and Coventry Climax, and
Britoil.[5] It had plans in 1983 for much more privatisation. In
addition, during its first term, it sold about half a million council
houses and flats. Public expenditure on housing, education and
environmental services dropped, whilst spending on health grew
more slowly than expenditure on the police (up nearly 25 per
cent in real terms, 1978/9–1982/3) and defence (which rose by
16·7 per cent in real terms between 1978/9 and 1982/3). Overall,
the Conservative administration had effected a considerable shift
in the direction of public policy.

But did 'U-turns' continue after 1979? Was the government
forced to renege on any of its election promises? Mrs Thatcher
remained adamant that there was to be no change in the government's economic strategy, a determination summed up in her
own words – 'You turn if you like, the lady's not for turning'. But
even if it did not consciously reverse its policy, the government
certainly did not carry out its manifesto intentions in two major
spheres. Rather than being reduced as intended, the burden of
taxation rose from 34 per cent of Gross Domestic Product (GDP)
in 1978–9 to nearly 40 per cent of GDP. Rather than falling as
desired, public expenditure rose as a proportion of GDP from 41
per cent in 1978–9 to 44 per cent in 1982–3. As a consequence of
increases in the numbers of pensioners, the unemployed and the
poor, social security spending rose by nearly 20 per cent between
1978–9 and 1982–3.[6] The government had some achievements to
its credit. It reduced the inflation rate (4·6 per cent in March
1983) by more than a half, negotiated the independence of
Rhodesia (Zimbabwe), gained a substantial refund from the
EEC of over £2·5 billion (1980–1983) and fought a successful war
to recapture the Falklands. Equally, it suffered some severe
setbacks. Between the second quarter of 1979 and the final
quarter of 1982, GDP fell by 4·2 per cent. Between May 1979
and February 1983, industrial production declined by 10·2 per
cent and manufacturing production by 17·3 per cent. Unemployment rose by about 2 million during the lifetime of the government.[7] By early 1983 real personal disposable income was at

about the same level as in the spring of 1979. The country had not been turned round. The effectiveness of British Government had not increased.

Finally, how did the advent of the Conservatives in 1979 change relationships between government and the big sectional (and other) groups? Under previous Conservative and Labour administrations, dating back to the early 1960s, a 'corporate' philosophy of joint economic management between government, business and unions had held sway. The Conservative Government rejected tripartism, leaving both the CBI and the TUC out in the cold. Both were much reduced in status, but neither could do anything about it. When manufacturing industry suffered in the recession, the government took no action to assist as a strong pound sterling handicapped the capacity of exporters to sell British goods abroad. Moreover, as has been seen in chapter 5, the government brought trade union rights and privileges under legislative attack, proceeding cautiously and gradually this time, not hastily as Heath had done. In addition, by its policies of cash limits, privatisation and resolute resistance to strikes in the public sector, it sought to weaken the bargaining position and disruptive capability of the public sector unions. Between 1980 and 1982, the government successfully resisted the steel, rail, civil service and health service unions in a series of disputes. In a context of falling membership, mass redundancies and closures, union militancy evaporated. Three times, as already noted, the miners voted against strike action. Managerial control was restored at British Leyland, and the government worked to create a 'climate' favourable to its restoration elsewhere. Facing the 'squeeze' on public sector spending, campaigning pressure groups such as Shelter and Child Poverty Action had less scope. On the other hand, simple protest flared up, both spontaneous and organised, both within and outside the bounds of legality. During the spring and summer of 1981, riots with a racial complexion exploded in major cities, notably Bristol, London (Brixton) and Liverpool (Toxteth). CND organised protest against governmental defence policy. Some groups went in for civil disobedience, either non-violent like the Greenham Common women or violent like some animal rights campaigners. The Animal Liberation Front raided factory farms and experimental laboratories, releasing animals and damaging property; the animal rights militia delivered a letter bomb to Downing Street. The main changes since the 1970s were clear. Whilst remaining vigorous, the major sectional and campaigning groups have lost influence at the highest levels of public policy-making, but new campaigning and protest groups have emerged and older campaigns been revived, for example, CND.

Government is still *party* government but the party in office now shares its effective power with the minor parties and extra-parliamentary groups to a much greater extent than in the immediate post-war period. This system is best described as a blend of territorial and functional representation, although much discussion of the roles of parties and groups continues to assume the existence of complete parliamentary sovereignty. Parties, of course, fit comfortably inside that legal and political framework: pressure groups do so to a much lesser extent. The most important criticisms of the contemporary political system will now be examined, although some issues, such as electoral reform and the workings of the civil service, clearly fall outside the present discussion.

Criticisms and replies
There are three significant criticisms of the roles of parties and pressure groups in the contemporary system of government. The first of these argues that British Government in the last two decades has often been ineffective because the claims of party are pushed too far. There are really two points being made here, one relatively minor, the other of major importance. The comment is often heard, first, that parties make decisions for their own short-term benefit which damage the national interest. The 1975 referendum on the EEC, held not because it was necessary but in order to prevent a serious split in the Labour Party, is a good example. But the major worry is that important economic decisions are constantly being made in response to short-term electoral considerations. This practice is undesirable in economic terms since pre-election booms are usually followed by deflationary policies and politically because it leads to public cynicism and thereby discredits the system as a whole. This criticism of the present behaviour of parties is true, and damaging. But there are

counter-balancing factors. For parties to act for their own self-preservation and advantage is neither novel nor avoidable. If manipulation of the economy by the governing party were to prevent their opponents ever winning power, the count would be much more serious. In fact, it does not, as witness for example, the elections of 1970 and 1979. Party rivalry in this case is carried too far but on balance the political and economic 'costs' may be a small price to pay for a competitive (as opposed to a monolithic) party system.

The second criticism maintains that Britain's political system has become one of 'adversarial politics'.[8] Instead of looking for support in the 'moderate' centre ground of politics, the two major parties – especially when in opposition – drift towards the extreme ends of the political spectrum. Having secured electoral victory, they then use their political power to foist their extreme policies on the nation. Each side by policy and legislation rewards its own leading groups of supporters – for example, the Conservatives favour business and finance; Labour, the trade unions. Above all, each party uses its power to reverse major policies of its predecessor. Such political behaviour exaggerates class rivalry and produces violent swings of policy especially on such vital issues as the management of the economy and the boundary between public and private ownership. In addition, it forces issues which have little to do with traditional party differences into a party mould – for example, the EEC, immigration and devolution. As has already been noted in this chapter, there is a degree of truth in this contention. In the 1970s and 1980s, under the influence of a revival of ideological thinking, the major parties did move strongly right and left, reverse each other's policies and more or less blatantly operate to advantage their 'natural' supporters. But does this description characterise the entirety of their conduct, or only some of it?

In fact, the argument underestimates the extent of continuity between governments of opposed political complexions. If adversary politics were to prevail, each party in government could expect opposition from its political opponents on a high proportion of its legislation. However, this is not the case, There was no division of principle on 80 per cent of the government bills introduced by the 1970–1974 Conservative Government, and no division of principle on 77 per cent of the bills introduced by the 1974–1979 Labour Government.[9] In the first session of the 1979 Parliament – although party controversy increased – 63 per cent of Acts went through without divisions of principle.[10] The evidence suggests that even at times when party competition is especially intense, there is a considerable amount of continuity between the rival parties in office. Monetarist policy, as has been seen, began under the Labour Government in 1976. In the war against Argentina in 1981 for the recapture of the Falklands, the Conservative Government had the support of both Labour and the Alliance. In practice, government is shaped by many factors, including not only party but also the civil service and external pressures. The claims of party are on occasion pushed too far, often with damaging effects. But the adversary politics thesis – that this is entirely or largely the case and that it is the primary reason for the ineffectiveness of British Government – cannot be sustained.

A third significant criticism of the contemporary system of government concerns the role of pressure groups. The three most frequently-voiced adverse comments are: first, that the major sectional groups wield too much power; second, that there is inequality of influence between the organised and non-organised and amongst the organised groups themselves; and third, that some groups resort to the tactics of militant direct action which is unacceptable in a democratic community. Each of these points is considered in turn.

The first criticism maintains that during the 1970s, key political decisions, especially in the management of the economy, were made by the party in government in concert with the peak organisations of workers and employers. This corporatist tripartite division of power, two parts of which represented sectional interests and only one of which consisted of MPs, had the effect of displacing parliament from the centre of the political stage. The governing party proposes; the TUC and CBI dispose; parliament is then informed, but its assent to whatever has been decided is a virtual formality. MPs have little real power against the large producer organisations. This is to be deplored not only because it bypasses the democratically-elected assembly but also because it undermines the effectiveness of government. As well as positive power to shape government to their ends the major groups held a vote over what they did not want, with adverse effects upon economic growth, in particular. As countervailing power, the big sectional groups were able to prevent government attaining nationally-desirable goals.

This argument has been heard much less often in the 1980s after the advent to power of Mrs Thatcher with her domination over the two main producer groups. But even in the 1970s the view that the influence of the groups had become too great was selective; it exaggerated their successes and played down their failures. In reality, both failure and success attend group activity: the TUC and the CBI, both then and in the 1980s, usually got some but not all of their requests accepted by government. The TUC (down to 1977) had failed to persuade the government to invest £1 billion in private enterprise and to make planning agreements with companies compulsory rather than voluntary. Its persistent opposition to incomes policies and pay pauses was also frequently ignored. Indeed, in 1973, two writers described the trade unions as 'a relatively unsuccessful pressure group.[11] Perhaps their period of considerable influence (from 1973 to 1976) was a particular historical phase, a reaction to the preceding attempts by successive governments to legislate for industrial relations. After 1976 TUC influence appeared to decrease; it failed both to prevent cuts in projected public expenditure and to persuade the government to introduce selective import controls. Moreover, the influence of the CBI in the ten years after its formation in 1965 was less marked than that of the TUC; a study written in 1977 concluded that it had had 'little consistent direct influence over the policies pursued by government'.[12] Despite occasional spectacular gains for its members (e.g. massive tax relief on stock appreciation in 1974 and revisions to the price code worth £1,000 million to company profits in 1976), the CBI failed to prevent the renationalisation of Iron and Steel in 1967 and its consistent preference for voluntary prices and incomes policies was often ignored by governments. Detailed benefits won for members were not accompanied by an influence on broad economic policy.

Several factors limit the influence of the CBI and TUC. First, the Government remains the ultimate arbiter: in a system of competing élites, the political élite predominates. It is armed with powerful weapons against the demands of any sectional interest group. These include the very specialised, technical expertise of ministers and civil servants, a knowledge of public opinion on any particular issue as expressed by the polls and the terms laid down for the management of the British economy by foreign bankers as a condition of their loans (for example the £2 million cuts in projected public expenditure demanded by the International Monetary Fund in December 1976). Second, in a collaborative relationship, discussions more often produce compromise than a 'victory' for any 'side'. Both in dealings with each other and with the government, the TUC and CBI are constantly forced to modify their own positions. Thus between 1975 and 1977 the TUC came to accept that wage inflation was a major cause of unemployment and that higher profits were needed to stimulate business confidence, boost investment and increase job prospects. Finally, business and unions have to compete for influence with other important interest groups. The financial institutions of the City (large banks, insurance companies and the Stock Exchange) rival them as a source of political influence. The CBI is itself challenged by organisations such as the Retail Consortium, the Association of British Chambers of Commerce, the British Institute of Management and the Institute of Directors.

The claim that pressure groups exert excessive influence is therefore 'not proven'. This does not mean that the sum of sectional interests may be identified with the national interest in any specific instance. What may in a broader sense be claimed to be in the national interest is the system of pluralism itself. For bargaining between important groups is a more democratic and potentially effective way to conduct politics than a simple command-obedience relationship between parliament and the rest. Agreements made between government and interest groups are not necessarily opposed to the wishes of parliament. In any case, the decline of parliamentary sovereignty has been exaggerated. Parliament has never been a governing body, but rather a forum for criticism and debate. Nor has parliamentary influence been completely set aside. The ruling party remains responsible to parliament. Indeed, the Labour Government of October 1974 became dependent on the support of the Liberal Party in parliament, and this gave Liberal leaders political influence comparable to that of prominent trade unionists and industrialists alike.

It would be fair to conclude therefore that a single sectional interest is not able consistently or habitually to impose its will on government at the expense of the public interest. Nor are several groups acting together able to do this. Furthermore, any assessment of 'too much influence' is always to some extent a subjective matter, sectional interests may coincide with the national interest as well as compete with it, and in practice it is not always easy to say whether or not the government has acted as a result of the pressure of a particular group. Moreover, while the influence of groups upon government is not always beneficial, it has also to be remembered that the achievement of greater legitimacy by groups is both a symptom and a condition of a free society and an indication of the responsiveness of the political system to developing social needs.

A second criticism of the pressure group system is that the sum total of their efforts leads to a situation of inequality of influence between sections of the community which are organised and those which are not. It also benefits the larger groups, especially those with industrial 'muscle', against the smaller ones, which lack the capacity to threaten disruption. Examples are not far to seek. Nationally, the TUC speaks for the employed; the nearly four million unemployed have no effective voice despite being allowed to attend the TUC conference in 1982. At the local level, a similar kind of criticism can be made of the activity of pressure groups, despite the good they do. Thus, the term 'community action' became popular in the decade after 1965 to describe a wide variety of efforts to mobilise the deprived to protect their own interests in a particular neighbourhood. It is an attempt to overcome the defects of the formal system of representative local government. Claimants' unions, tenants' associations, neighbourhood councils and residents' associations have sprung up alongside a host of action groups dedicated to specific goals such as keeping open footpaths, improving road crossings and providing nursery schools. Yet, in spite of its undoubted achievements, this type of pressure groups activity is inevitably selective in its coverage. One area, for example, may possess a residents' action group to press its welfare and housing claims; another, perhaps equally deserving, does not. Some districts are more likely to generate successful action groups than others. Moreover, a victory is sometimes won by one group at the expense of other sections of the community. For example, residents of Carlton and West Bridgford in Nottinghamshire successfully campaigned for the resiting of a power station at Ratcliffe-on-Soar in 1963; but the inhabitants of Long Eaton, Beeston and Stapleford, who lived near the relocated station, suffered because they came within close range of atmospheric pollution.

Again, so far as inequality of influence is concerned, workers in 'key industries' (coal mining, electricity supply) have an advantage over the majority whose work is not absolutely essential to national survival. And if it is objected that the National Union of Mineworkers had made little progress against the Conservative Government by January 1985, at least it may be said that the miners had the option of resistance when their jobs were threatened. Most workers in that situation have no such possibility. Clearly, there are still considerable inequalities between groups and sections of society: producers are more strongly represented than consumers, pensioners than parents. All groups in the community do not enjoy parity of access to, let alone influence over, government.

This inequality of influence is both true, and, in a free society, also unavoidable. It reflects amongst other things the differing sizes, coherence, strategic importance, persistence and quality of leadership of the different groups in society. So long, it may be said, as there is no formal obstacle to the establishment and activities of groups, so long as no section of the community is legally prevented from pressing its case, there can be no possibility of equality of influence. Moreover, it is also necessary to remember the positive case for pressure group activity at all levels of society. Pressure groups are vital to democratic government. They facilitate the control of governments; enable popular grievances to be brought into the open, and remedied; express and protect the views of minorities; provide alternative perspectives to those presented by the civil service; keep important issues constantly in the public mind, compared with the transience of media attention; and generally raise the quality of political debate.

Lastly, some groups have been criticised for their use of militant direct action methods. In the early 1970s, aggressive pressure group tactics stopped the proposed tour of the South African cricket team as a protest against apartheid; helped to bring victory in the miners' strike (of 1971); and, in 1974, destroyed the power-sharing executive in Northern Ireland. In the 1980s, although with less success, animal rights campaigners also used violent direct action. Such conduct was engaged in by a very few extremists, condemned by the vast majority of people and seemed decreasingly effective as governments learnt to withstand the far greater violence employed by terrorists.

Clearly, in so far as contemporary British Government is ineffective, its inadequacies cannot all be laid at the door of parties and pressure groups. Nonetheless, they do not emerge entirely unscathed from such criticisms, as has been seen. This chapter concludes by examining two proposals to remedy two defects which, if anything, became worse in the 1980s. The whole system suffered, it has been suggested, from the weakness of political opposition and from the fact that government was minority government, supported by only just over two-fifths of voters and under one-third of the electorate.

Proposals to improve the effectiveness of government have concentrated on the need to strengthen parties *in opposition* and on the probable advantages of *coalition government* over the system of single-party government. After more than a decade of reforms, it is recognised that new institutions are unlikely to prove a general panacea. It remains important to achieve the right machinery of government but it is the politicians themselves and the constraints within which they work which probably have a greater influence upon long-term results.

Strengthening the major opposition party might improve government in two ways. First, it would provide a more effective challenge to the government and thus help to improve its performance; second, it would enable the opposition party, as a potential government, to produce better legislative proposals. At present, despite state assistance for the opposition parties, a glaring disparity exists between the kind of resources for policy-formation which are available to a party in government and those to which it has access in opposition. The government commands the entire resources of the civil service whereas the opposition has merely the inadequate facilities available to backbenchers – small groups of Research Department staff together with whatever other assistance might be provided by private bodies like the Rowntree Trust. One possible antidote to the vagueness and ideological extremism of parties in opposition might be to increase their contacts with civil servants or even to provide them with their own embryo civil service by seconding administrators to them on a permanent basis. Parties could also be assisted by parliamentary draftsmen in formulating the details of legislative proposals.

The likely success of these suggestions depends on the reasons for the defects of the parties in opposition. In so far as their failings are political rather than administrative or financial, the problem may be less amenable to solution by such straightforward measures. For example, parties may accept the disadvantages which they face in opposition as the necessary price for their own expected invulnerability in government. There may be a certain amount of inter-party collusion to keep government strong. Moreover, whereas the party in office lacks an incentive to strengthen the opposition, the party in opposition lacks the power. Equally, the style of party manifestoes may result from a combination of a tactical desire to avoid firm commitments, the greater influence of backbench and extra-parliamentary party pressures in opposition and the diminished force of appeals to 'moderation'. Finally, as after 1983, the numerical weakness of the main opposition party may severely limit its potential influence.

Proponents of coalition government argue that it would be just as strong as, or even stronger than, one-party government in parliament through its possession of a secure majority, and that it would have a much stronger base amongst the electorate. A combination of two parliamentary parties in government would command the support of approximately 60 per cent of the voters rather than the 37 per cent and 39 per cent gain by Labour in the two elections of 1974 or the 44 per cent and 42·5 per cent won by the Conservatives in 1979 and 1983. Thus in electoral terms minority governments would be transformed into majority governments. Such a wide consensus would be invaluable in controversial areas of policy such as incomes and industrial relations. At the same time, if the largest party after an election were forced to negotiate with the leading minor party over the terms of its parliamentary support, governments might be less prone to ideological extremes or to sweeping reversals of their predecessor's policies.

Opponents of the idea contend that coalition blurs political responsibility. It removes decisions about policies from the electorate to parliament where haggling over the content of governmental programmes takes place *after* elections between party leaders. Nor is it always clear where responsibility for a particular measure lies. It is also alleged that coalition government slows down the decision-making process because of the continual need for agreement between two parties; two groups of backbenchers with widely differing prejudices have to be placated before anything can be done. Supporters of coalition government argue that it is not necessarily irresponsible, since the parties composing the coalition can be identified and the terms on which they agree can be made public. The Labour-Liberal agreement of 1977 may be seen as a limited form of coalition: the Liberal Party gave parliamentary support to Labour, but no Liberal took office.[13] In 1983 the Liberal and Social Democratic parties agreed on a joint programme to present to the electorate.

7 Parties, Pressure Groups and Democracy

Political participation

The contemporary political system has many advantages. It gives everyone some say in public decisions. It affords some choice between alternative policies and goals. In enables electors to assess the record of governments periodically and to bring them to account. It gives business and the trade unions rather than the official opposition party the capacity to veto the will of governments. It encourages rulers to pursue the public interest, although, as we have seen, with apparently diminishing effectiveness. Yet the phrase 'representative and responsible government through parliamentary institutions' now seems to many political observers an inadequate description of the system. 'Elective autocracy tempered by oligarchic pluralism' offers a more realistic and less complacent assessment of British political institutions. The liberal-democratic ideal demands not only a role for the individual in political decision-making but also increased opportunities for *participation* and a greater degree of *choice*. This chapter begins by assessing party and pressure group democracy in the United Kingdom in the light of these two criteria.

For most people, voting in elections is the sum total of their participation in politics. About three-quarters of the electorate (73 per cent in 1983) votes in general elections and about 40 per cent in local elections. Of course, this minimal involvement may have great significance for the system as a whole and the importance of the act of voting both for government and citizens in a democracy is often underestimated. A survey conducted in 1969 found that 46 per cent of people thought that having elections made the government pay a 'good deal' of attention to public opinion; 26 per cent thought that elections made the government pay 'some' attention; and only 16 per cent considered that elections had little effect on the actions of government.[1] Whether people are right to consider that elections make rulers so responsive is less clear, although reports of conversations between politicians would seem to suggest that they do. Nonetheless, however great their political importance, elections still make only minimal demands on the individual.

Only a small minority of the population have a greater political involvement: a mere 5 per cent of the electorate are individual members of political parties and an even smaller proportion are party 'activists'. Fewer still can reasonably hope to serve their party in parliament. There were 2,577 parliamentary candidates in 1983 for only 650 seats.[2] In 1973 local government reorganisation reduced the number of local councillors from 40,000 to 24,000.[2] Moreover, membership of the major political parties has shown a gradual yet persistent decline since 1945, and does not appear to have been offset by gains for the smaller parties; these have certainly taken votes from the major parties but not, it seems, their members.[3]

Many people from the 1960s on probably joined pressure groups instead. This period witnessed an explosion of pressure group activity. In the early 1980s, the environmental and peace movements became major social phenomena; between 2·5 and 3 million people belonged to environmental groups in 1981,[4] and CND had 100,000 national and 400,000 local members in 1984. Animal welfare groups also expanded rapidly; membership of the British Union for the Abolition of Vivisection rose from 2,500 to 14,000 between 1980 and 1982. This increase in numbers is very significant: for social reformers, protesters and for those who simply wanted to protect their own interests, pressure groups had become a genuine and attractive alternative to political parties.

If pressure group membership is included as political activity, political participation increases, although it is hard to say by how much. As with party memberships, members of pressure groups exhibit varying degrees of commitment from intense activity to the mere payment of dues. More significantly, voluntary groups may not be politically orientated. In their book, *The Civic Culture*, Gabriel Almond and Sidney Verba reported the following findings. Nearly half the population in Great Britain (47 per cent) belonged to some organisation or other but less than one-fifth (19 per cent) belonged to an organisation which they considered to be involved in politics. The largest category of organisations to which people belonged (29 per cent) consisted of economic groups, such as trade unions (22 per cent), business (4 per cent) and professional associations (3 per cent), many of which, of course, should be seen as deeply politicised. But this leaves many other groups, such as social, charitable and religious organisations (21 per cent of group membership), some of which may be completely non-political. Fewer people were 'activists'. Only 13 per cent of the population, and 29 per cent of group members, had held office in an organisation.[5]

The level of political participation varies considerably over time; at times of heightened political controversy it will obviously increase. The CND campaign against nuclear weapons in the late 1950s and again in the early 1980s and the TUC campaign against the 1971 Industrial Relations Act generated great political excitement and exceptional activity: many people who would usually stand on the political sidelines marched and demonstrated. S.E. Finer has offered an analysis of opposition to the 1947 Transport Act based on the notion of secondary density – that is, the ratio of people actively involved in a campaign to the total electorate. Opposition to this Act spread beyond the organised interests which were affected to include ordinary members of the public, but even on the most favourable estimate, the campaign did not involve more than 10 per cent of the electorate.[6]

The conclusion is clear. Although pressure groups increased in legitimacy at the expense of political parties after the mid-1960s, most citizens are not active members of either type of organisation. Of course, it is not easy to say what proportion of citizens would have to be active in politics before the system could be said to be working democratically. Furthermore, how is 'active involvement' to be defined? Nevertheless, even on minimal criteria, it is hard to be satisfied with the present working of British democracy and some possible ways of increasing participation are considered later in this chapter.

But first we turn to some related considerations. If parties and groups are imperfect as agencies of political participation, how representative are their leaderships and how democratic is their internal organisation? In a democracy, the members of voluntary groups like parties ought to have some say in their running, otherwise what point is there in joining them? And powerful organisations such as pressure groups, which do not usually present themselves for election, ought to be able to show that they reflect the real wishes of their members.

The internal organisation of both major parties was discussed in chapter 3. The conclusion was drawn that despite their very considerable differences and Labour's ostensibly more democratic structure, the assumption of governmental office in practice places formidable power in the hands of both leaderships. Attempts to make the political parties more democratic have focused on leadership election procedure, the role of party conferences in policy-making and the relationship between constituency activists and their Members of Parliament. Party practice varies at present. Ordinary members elect the leader of the SDP and Liberal parties, but the Labour Party leader is elected by an electoral college of trade unionists, MPs and constituency parties and the Conservative Party leader by MPs only. Labour, the Liberals and the SDP accord a more significant role in policy making to their representative bodies than do the Conservatives. Only Labour practices mandatory re-selection of MPs, but it is the management committees who decide, not the local membership.

However, to extend participation in the selection of leaders and MPs to party 'activists' alone rather than to entire party memberships is not necessarily to make the political system as a whole more democratic. Party activists not only constitute a very small minority of the population, they are also unrepresentative. There is a paradox here. If parties become 'more responsive to the opinion of their activists', they will also become more 'extreme' and therefore less valuable as mechanisms of democracy. Such a trend could contribute to the further electoral decline of the two major parties, as each became decreasingly able to reflect the attitudes and opinions of ordinary moderate voters. It might also lead to an intensification of adversary politics with all its attendant problems.

The representativeness of pressure group leaderships, especially of spokesmen for the large producer groups, became a matter of intense political concern after 1965. Inevitably perhaps, in a period when the Labour Party was in power, attention in the mid-1970s focused on the trade union movement. But similar questions about representativeness can and should be asked about the spokesmen of any sectional or promotional group.

With reference to trade unionism, three points received special emphasis: the extent to which the formal links between the trade union movement and the Labour Party reflected the views of the rank-and-file trade unionists; the degree to which union leaders spoke for their members' actual opinions on important political and industrial issues; and the degree of rank-and-file control over the selection and activities of union leaderships.

The strong financial and constitutional links between the unions and the Labour Party have already been indicated. But this relationship is hardly representative of the political opinions of ordinary trade unionists. In the 1983 general election, according to MORI, 60 per cent of trade unionists voted for the two other major parties (31 per cent Conservative, 29 per cent Alliance), only 39 per cent for Labour.[7] The Communist Party, which, as we have seen, has had very little electoral success since 1951, is disproportionately well represented on union executives. Of the 345 executive members of the thirteen largest trade unions, between forty and fifty support the Communist Party; the remaining 87 per cent are Labour Party supporters. Overall, it has been estimated that 10 per cent of union officials are communists.[8] Studies of individual unions tend to confirm these differences in political attitude between leaderships and rank-and-file. A study of the Union of Post Office Workers, for example, showed that most ordinary members thought that the union should be primarily concerned with securing better pay and conditions for its members and that 'a substantial number – perhaps a majority' were, from the foundation of the union, 'unenthusiastic about forging links with the rest of the Labour Movement'. By contrast, for the activist minority, joining the union was a product of their political commitment to the workers' cause and to the establishment of a socialist society.[9]

There is widespread support for greater union democracy. In a *Times*/ORC public opinion poll published in January 1981, 85 per cent of the sample considered that there should be secret ballots before strikes and 73 per cent thought that trade union leaders should be elected by secret ballot.[10] Strike ballots held in the early 1970s confirmed strike decisions taken at the national level: railwaymen in 1972 and miners in 1973 and 1974 supported their leaders' decisions. In the late 1970s and early 1980s, however, strike ballots have gone the other way. The miners voted three times against strike action between 1981 and 1983 (see p. 125). In 1979, BL balloted the workforce on its Recovery Plan when this was rejected by the unions and the workforce voted 7:1 in favour of the Plan in a secret ballot conducted by the Electoral Reform Society.[11] Moreover, the sketchy evidence that exists on matters of social and economic policy suggests that union leaders and rank-and-file members often disagree. Those leaders who opposed statutory incomes policies and the Industrial Relations Court, fought entry to Europe and supported further nationalisation came into conflict with large numbers, often majorities, of their memberships on these issues.[12]

In some unions, the chief officer (the General Secretary) is elected by a ballot of members, but the fact of election is generally offset by the appointment being for life and by the very low poll, often in the region of 10 per cent, in union elections. Also, some methods of election are more satisfactory than others. For example, the postal ballot in the AUEW is more likely to be an accurate representation of unionists' preferences than the conduct of elections in branch meetings (e.g. by a 'show of hands'). Officials below the General Secretary are normally appointed by union executives although a model democracy like the engineering section of the AUEW is exceptional in electing all its officials. The unions' accountability to their members, therefore, is hardly adequate. This is not always because the necessary democratic procedures are lacking; in fact, many union rule-books afford their members an opportunity to overturn decisions, to hold their leaders to account and even to get rid of them. In the UPW, however, despite its democratic structure, Moran found that 'few members use these mechanisms; the prevailing calculative attitudes result in very limited interest and participation, and in little knowledge of important union policies'. Hence, the small minority who run the union have a great deal of freedom in deciding what its goals should be, and demands such as that for a closed shop, which few members supported, could nonetheless be decided in a democratic manner and 'presented as the expressed wish of the members'.[13] The overall picture, perhaps, is not surprising. People join unions for the material benefits they are thought to bring and normally take little interest in how they are run and what their general policies are, but on matters which concern them very much, pay, for example, they can and often do assert their viewpoint strongly. Many a national trade union leader has been confronted by resistance from a rank-and-file membership unwilling to be led where he wants them to go.[14]

The 1984 Trade Union Act will undoubtably have a considerable impact on union procedures (see page 135 for its main provisions on the balloting of members). A survey of the twenty largest TUC-affiliated unions conducted by *The Guardian* showed that over half were going to have to make radical changes if they were to avoid the threat of court action by employers or dissident members.[15] Already by late 1984 a company had invoked the Act against a trade union. When the TGWU supported a strike at Austin-Rover on the basis of a show of hands at mass meetings, the company sought and obtained an injunction under the 1984 Trade Union Act. This injunction instructed the union not to encourage or to persuade its members to strike over pay. The Act removed the unions' immunity from civil action if it called a strike without first holding a secret ballot. When the TGWU refused to comply with the injunction it was fined £200,000.

Problems of the accountability of leaders and officials to their memberships are common to all large organisations. They extend also to the CBI, which has sometimes been accused of being an 'irresponsible oligarchy', unrepresentative of the many thousands of firms for whom it claims to speak. Like the major political parties and the TUC, the CBI is a coalition of diverse interests, attitudes and opinions which cannot easily be added together to produce a uniform consensus. Nevertheless, despite its internal tensions, the authors of the first full-length study of the CBI conclude that it is 'not an oligarchy. The leading permanent officials and committee chairmen certainly have a great deal of influence over the course taken by the organisation, but their freedom of manoeuvre is limited by the fact that they must pursue policies broadly acceptable to the majority of CBI members'.[16]

Yet the discussion of 'representativeness' and 'accountability' must include more than the right of members to reject leaders with whose policies they disagree or to challenge them on the floors of conference halls. It is not sufficient simply to point to the existence of some democratic *procedures*. Low rates of participation destroy the legitimacy of parties and pressure groups alike as agencies of representation and of government. The real options available to citizens may need to be greatly extended in order for the system to merit the term 'democratic' in the last quarter of the twentieth century.

Suggested reforms

There are two possible responses to the levels of citizen participation in parties and pressure groups examined so far. One is simply to say that they are too low and should be increased. The other is to take the problem of this apparent apathy more seriously and to ask about the underlying reasons for it. Each approach is based on a different conception of participatory democracy and each has different implications for institutional reform.

The case for an increase in citizen-involvement in local and national government and at the workplace is straightforward. It rests upon the moral value of participation: it offers a restatement of the classical Greek idea that people will fail to develop their potential as moral beings if they do not participate fully in the affairs of the community. The implication of this argument is that every effort should be made to increase and strengthen participatory institutions. Membership drives should be launched in the political parties. People should be urged to take a more active part in pressure groups. Neighbourhood councils, parent-teacher associations and local inquiries into planning decisions should be encouraged. All these would make considerable demands on the ordinary citizen.

It may be, however, that in practice a less exacting conception of participation is more in keeping with the realities of modern society. The needs of industrial production and the likely preference of most citizens for a private rather than a public existence may call for a set of participatory institutions which make fewer demands on the energy, articulateness and resources of ordinary people than any of those so far created. This contention does not necessarily mean that citizens at present are lacking in civic spirit; it merely suggests that to people at work for upwards of forty hours every week the sacrifices required by serious political activity are just too great. Yet, at the same time, it remains important that government should take their wishes into account and that people should somehow be able to make choices for themselves rather than have choices made for them by civil servants, parties and groups. How can this be done?

A number of possibilities have been suggested. Primary elections on the American model would allow all members of a political party to participate in the election of their parliamentary candidates at relatively small cost to themselves in time and effort. It would also take candidate selection out of the hands of 'unrepresentative' groups of activists. Trade unions are already obliged by law to ballot their members to ascertain their views on controversial matters of policy, at a small cost in members' time. They are also being offered state financial assistance to hold postal ballots on offers on pay and conditions and on the continuation of their political funds. It might also be made compulsory for companies to ballot their shareholders on the political donations they make. In these ways, parties, pressure groups and other organisations can be made more representative and accountable.

Various other mechanisms could be used to counteract the imperfections of parties and pressure groups as registers of public opinion. Increasing use might be made of referenda. Market research surveys could be employed more widely to discover people's attitudes and preferences. Such devices would help government at all levels to elicit and to respond to the opinions and wishes of *all* the population. They would also serve to allay public suspicion that the major sectional interests and the more articulate promotional groups get too much of their own way.[17]

Governments could also help individuals to make better choices by providing more information. They could be less bland and secretive. Many of their reasons for secrecy are discreditable: two of the main ones are the desire to conceal previous mistakes and the fact that party interest frequently takes precedence over the public good. Election manifestoes and party political broadcasts tend to be patronising in tone and evasive in content. They and all other political communications could be improved by greater frankness; parties should spell out the real alternatives and the costs of their policies rather than promising 'something for nothing'. In other words, they should have the nerve and honesty to explain situations in the sort of language which political 'insiders' use in conversations between themselves. The two types of participatory democracy outlined above may be combined in a variety of ways. But however they complement one another, a democracy of information is an essential prerequisite of their success.

Notes and References

Chapter 1 Parties and Pressure Groups in British Politics

1. David Butler and Dennis Kavanagh, *The British General Election of 1983* (Macmillan, 1984). The following account draws upon this work and upon reports and analyses published in *The Guardian*.
2. Sidney Low, *The Governance of England* (Unwin, 1904).

Chapter 2 Parties and the Political System

1. Bo Sarlvik and Ivor Crewe, *Decade of Dealignment* (Cambridge University Press, 1983), pp. 333 and 314. See further ch. 2.
2. Richard Crossman, *The Diaries of a Cabinet Minister* (Hamish Hamilton and Jonathan Cape, 1975), 1, p. 50.
3. *Ibid.*, p. 90.
4. *The Politics of Education*, Edward Boyle and Anthony Crosland in conversation with Maurice Kogan (Penguin Education Special, 1971), p. 75.
5. Richard Rose, *Do Parties Make a Difference?* (Macmillan, expanded Second Edition, 1984), p. 65.
6. *Ibid.*, p. 66.
7. On the role of Opposition in British Politics, see R. M. Punnett, *Front-Bench Opposition* (Heinemann, 1973).
8. Peter G. Richards, *The Backbenchers* (Faber, 1972; 1974), p. 95.
9. Cited in Punnett, *op. cit.*, p. 253.
10. Philip Norton, *Dissension within the House of Commons* (Macmillan, 1975), pp. 609–613.
11. Philip Norton, *The Commons in Perspective* (Martin Robertson, 1981), pp. 609–613.
12. Rose, *op. cit.*, p. 79.
13. *Ibid.*, pp. 82–3.
14. J. A. G. Griffith, *Parliamentary Scrutiny of Government Bills* (Allen and Unwin, 1975).
15. Valentine Herman, 'Backbench and Opposition amendments to Government legislation', in Dick Leonard and Valentine Herman, eds., *The Backbencher and Parliament* (Macmillan, 1972), p. 148.

Chapter 3 The Conservative and Labour Parties

1. Allan Kornberg and Robert C. Frasure, 'Policy differences in British parliamentary parties', *American Political Science Review,* vol. 65, 3 (1971); 91 per cent of Conservative MPs opposed comprehensive schools whereas 92 per cent of Labour MPs supported them; 90 per cent of Conservatives were against a legally enforced prices and incomes policy but 51 per cent of Labour MPs supported one; and 83 per cent of Conservative MPs supported a continuing British military presence East of Suez while 91 per cent of Labour MPs opposed it.
2. 'British Social Attitudes', *Social and Community Planning Research* (1984).
3. David and Maurice Kogan, *The Battle for the Labour Party* (Kogan Page, 1982), p. 111.
4. Speeches of Roy Hattersley as reported in *The Guardian*, February 22, May 16 and September 24 1984.
5. Kogan and Kogan, *op. cit.,* p. 55.
6. Nigel Stanley, letter to *The Guardian*, December 22 1984.
7. See further Michael Crick, *Militant* (Faber and Faber, 1984), to which much of this section is indebted. Crick interestingly compares (pp. 128–130) Militant's annual income of over £1 million with the SDP's £1·25 million (1981–2), the Liberals' £1·5 million (1982) and with the very much smaller incomes of Labour groups – e.g. the Fabian Society's £81,000 (1982–3), *Tribune's* £140,000 (1980–1) and the Campaign for Labour Democracy's £14,494 (1982–3). The size of Militant's full-time staff (over 130 in 1983) also compares favourably with that of the Labour Party (about 200), the Liberal Party (about 50) and the SDP (about 30) (pp. 102–103).
8. Sir Keith Joseph, 'Monetarism is not enough', *Centre for Policy Studies.*
9. *The Guardian*, 16 April 1984.
10. Philip Vander Elst, 'Radical Toryism – the libertarian alternative', *Political Quarterly*, vol. 46, (1975).
11. Philip Norton and Arthur Aughey, *Conservatives and Conservatism* (Temple Smith, 1981), pp. 235–6.
12. *The Guardian*, 15 February 1984.
13. Robert Harris, *The Making of Neil Kinnock* (Faber and Faber, 1984), pp. 162–3.
14. *Ibid.*, pp. 237–8.
15. Quoted in Anthony King and Anne Sloman, *Westminster and Beyond* (Macmillan, 1973), p. 108.
16. 'Political Britain', *The Economist* (1980), p. 19. The idea of this

relationship between voters, leaders and activists first appeared in David Butler, 'The paradox of party difference' (1960), reprinted in Richard Rose, ed., *Studies in British Politics* (Macmillan, 1976); cf. Norton and Aughey, *op. cit.*, pp. 217 and 272, who dispute its relevance to the Conservative Party.

17. R. T. McKenzie, *British Political Parties* (Heinemann, rev. edn., 1964), pp. 151–2.
18. Butler and Kavanagh, *op. cit.*, pp. 227–8.
19. Austin Ranney, 'Selecting the candidates', in Howard R. Penniman, ed., *Britain at the Polls* (American Enterprise Institute for Public Policy, 1975), pp. 43–4.
20. The local party membership refused its assent at Southport in 1952 and before the 1968 by-election at Nelson and Colne; see M. Rush, 'Candidate selection and its impact on leadership recruitment', in J. D. Lees and R. Kimber, eds., *Political Parties in Modern Britain* (Routledge and Kegan Paul, 1972), p. 98. The Conservatives, however, did face problems as a result of the radical boundary revisions in 1983. On the scramble for new seats by fourteen MPs after October 1982, see Butler and Kavanagh, *op. cit.*, pp. 227–9.
21. David Butler and Dennis Kavanagh, *The British General Election of October 1974* (Macmillan, 1975), p. 210.
22. Butler and Kavanagh, *British General Election of 1983*, p. 219.
23. Michael Pinto-Duschinsky, 'Will Politics take a pounding?', *The Times*, 4 January 1985.
24. Unions affiliate fewer members to the Party than pay their political levies to the union in order to avoid having too dominant a voice at the Party Conference, where the size of a union's block vote is determined by the number of members it affiliates.
25. Membership of the political parties is hard to estimate precisely. The most reliable guide is the *Report of the Committee on Financial Aid to Political Parties* (Houghton Committee Report, Cmnd 6601, HMSO 1976). The Committee suggested that average memberships of constituency parties in 1974 were: Conservative 2,400; Labour, 500; Liberal, 300. These figures indicate national memberships of: Conservative, 1,495,000; Labour, 311,500; Liberal, 186,900. For a summary of the Report, see *The Economist*, 28 August 1976.
26. The Houghton Committee estimated that, if 5p were to be allocated to the parties for every vote received, on the basis of votes cast in the October 1974 general election, the two major parties would receive about £500,000 each, the Liberal Party about £250,000 and the other parties varying amounts below £50,000.

Chapter 4. The Minor Parties

1. For an interesting discussion, see, A. Michie and S. Hoggart, *The Pact, the inside story of the Lib-Lab. government, 1977–8* (Quartet Books, 1978), ch. 11.
2. Hugh Stephenson, *Claret and Chips* (M. Joseph, 1983), Introduction. See further Ian Bradley, *Breaking the Mould?* (Martin Robertson, 1981) for a perceptive interpretation of the SDP.
3. James G. Kellas, *The Scottish Political System* (Cambridge University Press, 1973), ch. 1.
4. Butler and Kavanagh, *British General Election of October 1974*, pp. 70–1.
5. Gordon Wilson, 'The Scottish National Party', in Hardiman Scott, ed., *How shall I vote?* (Bodley Head, 1976). See also W. A. Roger Mullin, 'The Scottish National Party', in H. M. Drucker, ed., *Multi-Party Britain* (Macmillan, 1979).
6. Dafydd Thomas, 'Plaid Cymru', in Hardiman Scott, *op. cit.* See also Denis Balsom, 'Plaid Cymru: the Welsh National Party', in Drucker, ed., *op. cit.*
7. Alan Butt Philip, *The Welsh Question* (University of Wales Press, 1975), p. 330.
8. Sarah Nelson, 'The Northern Ireland Parties', in Drucker, *op. cit.*, provides a useful introduction.
9. Martin Walker, *The National Front* (Fontana, 1977), pp. 78–83.
10. S. Taylor, *The National Front in English Politics* (Macmillan, 1982), p. 173.
11. No figures are published, and estimates vary: cf. Walker's figures, 20,000 to 14,000 (1973–9) with Taylor's 14,000 to 6,000 (1973–9).
12. Paul Wilkinson, *The New Fascists* (Pan, 1983), pp. 165–6.
13. Butler and Kavanagh, *British General Election of 1983*, p. 354.
14. John Gollan, 'The Communist Party', in Scott, *op. cit.*
15. John Tomlinson, *Left-Right* (John Calder, 1981) contains some useful information on these groups at pp. 61 *et seq.*
16. B. Baker, *The Far Left* (Weidenfeld and Nicolson, 1981), p. 61.
17. Butler and Kavanagh, *op. cit.*, p. 354.

Chapter 5 Pressure Groups

1. Stephen Kirby, 'Peace by piece: the Revival of anti-nuclear protest in Britain', *Teaching Politics*, vol. 12, no. 3, September 1983 and Paul Byrne and Joni Lovenduski, 'Two new protest groups: the Peace and Women's Movements', in H. Drucker *et al.*, eds., *Developments in British Politics* (Macmillan, 1983) provide valuable accounts of the Campaign for Nuclear Disarmament in the 1980s.

2. Michael Crick, *Scargill and the Miners* (Penguin Special, 1985), pp. 11–12.
3. *Ibid.*, pp. 149–50.
4. This section draws upon Wyn Grant and David Marsh, *The CBI* (Hodder and Stoughton, 1977).
5. 'Political Britain', *The Economist* (1980), pp. 24–5 contains a useful section on Government–Union relations since the war.
6. On these two promotional groups, see B. Frost and I. Henderson, 'Shelter', and J. Flewin, 'Cublington Airport', in Brian Frost, ed., *The Tactics of Pressure* (Galliard, 1975).
7. Richard Kimber and J. J. Richardson, *Pressure Groups in Britain* (Dent, 1974), p. 13.
8. M. Kogan, *Educational Policy-Making* (Allen & Unwin, 1975), p. 76.
9. William Plowden, *The Motor Car and Politics in Britain* (Pelican, 1971), p. 399.
10. Richards, *The Backbenchers*, pp. 192–3.
11. Quoted in A. H. Hanson and Malcolm Walles, *Governing Britain* (Fontana, rev. ed., 1975), p. 158.
12. Timothy C. May, *Trade Unions and Pressure Group Politics* (Saxon House, 1975), p. 33.
13. *The Economist*, 15 November 1975.
14. The Select Committee on Members' Interests (1969–70), cited in Richards, *The Backbenchers*, p. 180.
15. *The Observer*, 1 July 1984.
16. C. Hall, *How to Run a Pressure Group* (Dent, 1974).
17. Peter G. Richards, *Parliament and Conscience* (Allen & Unwin, 1970), p. 206.
18. 'The new corporate interest', reported in *The Guardian*, 5 April 1976.
19. R. Kimber and J. J. Richardson, eds., *Campaigning for the Environment* (Routledge and Kegan Paul, 1974), p. 99.
20. Keith Hindell and Madeleine Simms, 'How the abortion lobby worked', in Kimber and Richardson, *Pressure Groups in Britain*, pp. 160–1.
21. See p. 174 for an explanation of the notion of secondary density.
22. *Social Trends* (Central Statistical Office, 1985), p. 163; the figures of total union membership and percentage of total employees cited are for 1982.
23. See *The Guardian Directory of Pressure Groups and Representative Associations* (Wilton House Publications, 1976) for further evidence on group membership.

24. Richards, *Parliament and Conscience,* pp. 56; 84.
25. *Ibid,* pp. 102–3.

Chapter 6. Party and Pressure Group Government: Trends and Problems
1. Peter Self, 'Are we worse governed?' *New Society,* 19 May 1977.
2. S. Milligan, *The New Barons* (Temple Smith, 1976), p. 232.
3. Arthur Cyr, 'Current trends in British politics', *Parliamentary Affairs,* vol, 29, no. 1, (Winter, 1976).
4. A. Sked and C. Cook, *Post-War Britain* (2nd edn, 1984), pp. 321–2.
5. *Ibid.,* p. 339.
6. Peter Riddell, *The Thatcher Government* (Martin Robertson, 1983), pp. 112–4.
7. *Ibid.,* p. 78.
8. S. E. Finer ed., *Adversary Politics and Electoral Reform* (Anthony Wigram, 1975).
9. Rose, *Do Parties Make a Difference?,* p. 80.
10. *Ibid.,* p. xxvii.
11. Timothy May and Michael Moran, 'Trade unions as pressure groups', *New Society,* 6 September 1973.
12. Grant and Marsh, *The CBI,* p. 213.
13. For further discussion, see Rose, *Problem of Party Government,* pp. 120–9; 436–49 and Samuel Brittan, 'The economic contradictions of democracy', in Anthony King, ed., *Why is Britain becoming harder to govern?* (BBC, 1976).

Chapter 7 Parties, Pressure Groups and Democracy
1. David Butler and Donald Stokes, *Political Change in Britain* (Macmillan, 2nd edn, 1974), p. 29.
2. Butler and Kavanagh, *General Election of 1983,* p. 230.
3. 'Parties under pressure', 'Political Britain', *The Economist* (1976), p. 8.
4. P. Lowe and J. Goyder, *Environmental Groups in Politics* (Allen and Unwin, 1983).
5. Gabriel A. Almond and Sidney Verba, *The Civic Culture* (Little, Brown and Company (1963, 1965), pp. 244–64. For further evidence and analysis, see Robert Worcester, 'The hidden activists', in Richard Rose, *Studies in British Politics* (Macmillan, 1976, 3rd edn).
6. S. E. Finer, 'Groups and political participation', in G. Parry, ed., *Participation in Politics* (Manchester University Press, 1972).
7. See Table 2.4, p. 26.
8. Milligan, *op. cit.,* p. 223; see further Robert Taylor, *The Fifth Estate* (Pan, rev. edn, 1980), p. 122.

9. Michael Moran, *The Union of Post Office Workers* (Macmillan, 1974), pp. 107; 111.
10. Richard Clutterbuck, *Industrial Conflict and Democracy* (Macmillan, 1984), p. 24.
11. *Ibid.*, p. 95.
12. Milligan, *op. cit.*, pp. 218–222.
13. Moran, *op. cit.*, pp. 126; 136.
14. Taylor, *op. cit.*, ch. 6.
15. Patrick Wintour, 'How the Unions measure up to 'accountability'. *The Guardian*, 9 January 1984.
16. Grant and Marsh, *The CBI*, p. 104.
17. For further discussion, see Bernard Crick, 'Participation and the future of government', in J. A. G. Griffith, ed., *From Policy to Administration* (Allen and Unwin, 1975).

Select Bibliography

Chapter 1 Parties and Pressure Groups in British Politics
S. H. Beer, *Modern British Politics* (Faber 2nd, edn, 1969) is a brilliant historical account. K. Middlemass, *Politics in Industrial Society* (Deutsch, 1979) is a seminal study of the development of the twentieth century polity. A. J. Beattie, ed., *English Party Politics* (2 vols, Weidenfeld and Nicolson, 1970) is a collection of well-chosen documents, with excellent introductions to each section: vol. 2, *The Twentieth Century,* is particularly useful. G. Wootton, *Pressure Groups in Britain* (Allen Lane, 1975), is also a selection of documents set in an interpretative framework. D. Butler and D. Kavanagh, *The British General Election of 1983* (Macmillan, 1984), the twelfth in the series of Nuffield election studies, is an authoritative guide to the electoral behaviour of the parties.

Chapter 2 Parties and the Political System
The first three chapters of H. Drucker, P. Dunleavy, A. Gamble and G. Peele, eds., *Developments in British Politics* (Macmillan, 1983) provide a clear picture of recent trends. R. Rose, *The Problem of Party Government* (Macmillan, 1974; Pelican, 1976) is a stimulating and informative analysis which is also useful for chs. 1, 3, 4, 6 and 7. Recent electoral developments are analysed in depth in B. Sarlvik and I. Crewe, *Decade of Dealignment* (Cambridge University Press, 1983). On this theme, E. Hobsbawm puts forward a controversial argument in M. Jacques and F. Mulhearn, eds., *The Forward March of Labour Halted?* (Verso, 1981).

P. Norton, *The Commons in Perspective* (Martin Robertson, 1981) is a stimulating account. Philip Norton, *Dissension within the House of Commons, 1945–1974* (Macmillan, 1975) and *Conservative Dissidents, 1970–1974* (Maurice Temple Smith, 1978), are scholarly studies of intra-party dissent in the division lobbies; J. A. G. Griffith, *Parliamentary Scrutiny of Government Bills* (Allen & Unwin, 1975) examines the fate of amendments to government legislation in the late 1960s and early 1970s.

On opposition, G. Ponton, *Political Opposition* (Politics Association Occasional Publication, 4, 1976) provides a good brief survey. G. Ionescu and I. de Madariaga, *Opposition* (Pelican, 1972; first published, 1968) consider the subject at greater length while R. Barker, *Studies in Opposition* (Macmillan, 1971) has gathered together an interesting collection of readings. R. M. Punnett, *Front Bench Opposition* (Heinemann, 1973) surveys one-party opposition in Britain between 1945 and 1970.

Chapter 3 The Conservative and Labour Parties

P. Norton and A. Aughey, *Conservatives and Conservatism* (Temple Smith, 1981) and I. Gilmour, *Inside Right* (Quartet, 1978) are valuable on the Conservative Party. Useful works on the Labour Party include D. Kavanagh, ed., *The Politics of the Labour Party* (Allen and Unwin, 1982) and, on the internal feuds in the early 1980s, D. and M. Kogan, *The Battle for the Labour Party* (Kogan Page, 1982). R. Harris, *The Making of Neil Kinnock* (Faber and Faber, 1984) is a stimulating biography. P. Riddell, *The Thatcher Government* (Martin Robertson, 1983) is an excellent study and the same subject is covered from the perspective of the left in S. Hall and M. Jacques, eds., *The Politics of Thatcherism* (Lawrence and Wishart, 1983).

H. Pelling, *A Short History of the Labour Party* (Macmillan, 5th edn, 1976), D. Howell, *British Social Democracy* (Croom Helm, 1976), R. Blake, *The Conservative Party from Peel to Churchill* (Fontana, 1975, first published 1970) and T. F. Lindsay and M. Harrington, *The Conservative Party, 1918–1970* (Macmillan, 1974), cover the historical development of the two parties, M. Hatfield, *The House the Left Built* (Gollancz, 1978) and D. Coates, *Labour in Power?* (Longman, 1980), from a Marxist perspective, examine Labour in the 1970s. R. Behrens, *The Conservative Party from Heath to Thatcher* (Saxon House, 1979), A. Beattie, 'Macmillan's mantle: the Conservative Party in the 1970s', *Political Quarterly*, vol. 50, no. 3, July 1979, T. Russel, *The Tory Party: its policies, divisions and future* (Penguin, 1978) and N. Nugent and R. Bennett, eds., *The Political Right* (Saxon House, 1978) deal with the Conservative Party in the same period. Published work on the groups within the parties tends to date quickly, but Patrick Seyd, 'Factionalism in the 1970s', in Zig Layton-Henry, *Conservative Party Politics* (Macmillan, 1980) remains of value and M. Crick, *Militant* (Faber, 1984) is a well-researched study of a grouping on the left. The only real way to keep informed about the activities of the intra-party groups is through the columns of quality dailies such as *The Times* and *The Guardian* and weeklies such as *The Economist*.

The Report of the Committee on Financial Aid to Political Parties (The Houghton Report) (Cmnd. 6601, HMSO) contains authoritative information on party membership and finances in the mid-1970s. On the outside financial interests of Members, see Andrew Roth, *The Business Interests of MPs* (Parliamentary Profile Services, 1981), which will probably remain more accessible than the register kept after 1975 by parliament. Chapter 7 of Alan Doig, *Corruption and Misconduct in Contemporary British Politics* (Penguin, 1984) is also useful on this subject.

Chapter 4 The Minor Parties

H. Drucker, ed., *Multi-Party Britain* (Macmillan, 1979) contains informative chapters on the minor (as well as the major) parties, but does not include the SDP. I. Bradley, *Breaking the Mould?* is the best book to date on the SDP, which is also the subject of H. Stephenson, *Claret and Chips* (M. Joseph, 1981) and N. Tracy, *The Origins of the SDP* (Croom Helm, 1983) On the Liberal Party there are V. Bogdanor, *Liberal Party Politics* (Oxford University Press, 1983) and A. Cyr, *Liberal Party Politics in Britain* (Calder, 1977). A. Michie and S. Hoggart, *The Pact: the inside story of the Lib-Lab Government, 1977–8* (Quartet Books, 1978) is a valuable account. On the history of the party, there is C. Cook, *A Short History of the Liberal Party, 1900–1976* (Macmillan, 1976).

The extreme right is covered in M. Walker, *The National Front* (Fontana, 1977), N. Fielding, *The National Front* (RKP, 1981) and S. Taylor, *The National Front in English Politics* (Macmillan, 1982). J. Tomlinson, *Left-Right* (Calder, 1981) contains information on both political extremes. B. Baker, *The Far Left* (Weidenfeld and Nicolson, 1981) is useful on the extreme left. H. Pelling, *The British Communist Party* (A. and C. Black, 1958) is a historical account of its subject.

James G. Kellas, *The Scottish Political System* (Cambridge University Press, 1973), Alan Butt Philip, *The Welsh Question* (University of Wales Press, 1975) and J. Harbinson, *The Ulster Unionist Party, 1882–1973* (Blackstaff Press, 1973), provide valuable political and historical contexts against which to understand developments in Scottish and Welsh nationalism and Ulster Unionism. To these works should be added: J. Osmond, *Creative Conflict: the Politics of Welsh Devolution* (Routledge, 1978) and K. Webb, *The Growth of Nationalism in Scotland* (Pelican, 1978). The best brief account of the impact of Scottish and Welsh nationalism in the 1970s is H. Drucker and G. Brown, *The Politics of Nationalism and Devolution* (Longman, 1980).

Chapter 5 Pressure Groups

J. Richardson and A. Jordon, *Governing under Pressure* (M. Robertson, 1979) looks at pressure groups from the point of view of government and D. Wilson, *Pressure* (Heinemann, 1984) from the perspective of an experienced campaigner. R. Kimber and J. J. Richardson, eds., *Pressure*

Groups in Britain (Dent, 1974) contains a helpful introduction, a variety of studies of sectional and promotional groups in the 1950s and 1960s and some more general essays relating pressure groups to the political system.

On sectional groups, there are R. Taylor, *The Fifth Estate* (rev. edn., Pan, 1980) on the trade unions and Wyn Grant and David Marsh, *The CBI* (Hodder and Stoughton, 1977) on the leading business organisation. Wyn Grant and David Marsh also deal with retailing in 'The representation of retail interests in Britain', in *Political Studies*, 22, 1976. Section 5 of Anthony Sampson, *The Changing Anatomy of Britain* (Hodder and Stoughton, 1982) contains much useful information on the City in Part 3. On the relations between trade unions and governments in the 1960s and 1970s, there is D. Barnes and E. Reid, *Governments and Trade Unions* (Heinemann, 1980).

Information on the Campaign for Nuclear Disarmament may be sought in Paul Byrne and Joni Lovenduski, 'Two new Protest Groups: the Peace and Women's Movements', in H. Drucker *et al.*, eds., *op. cit.* and in J. Minnion and P. Bolsover, *The CND Story* (Alison and Busby, 1983). Some of the best studies of promotional groups are of environmental campaigns: for example, R. Kimber and J. J. Richardson, eds, *Campaigning for the Environment* (Routledge & Kegan Paul, 1974), Peter J. Smith, ed., *The Politics of Physical Resources* (Penguin, 1975) and P. Lowe and J. Goyder, *Environmental Groups in Politics* (Allen and Unwin, 1983). William Plowden, *The Motor Car and Politics in Britain* (Penguin, 1973) contains valuable insights into the relations between governments and the motor lobby. Patrick Seyd has written two valuable studies of campaigning groups in the field of welfare: 'Shelter: the national campaign for the homeless', *Political Quarterly*, vol. 46 (1975), and 'The Child Poverty Action Group', *Political Quarterly*, vol. 47 (1976). Frank Field, *Poverty and Politics* (Heinemann, 1982) tells the inside story of the CPAG's campaigns in the 1970s and Susanne MacGregor, *The Politics of Poverty* (Longman, 1981) sets the activities of organisations of and for the poor in the context of the development of national policy and ideas on poverty.

Bridget Pym, *Pressure Groups and the Permissive Society* (David & Charles, 1974) is a study of campaigning groups on moral issues in the 1960s which is well complemented by Peter G. Richards, *Parliament and Conscience* (Allen & Unwin, 1970), a consideration of these campaigns from a parliamentary perspective.

Chapter 6 Party and Pressure Group Government: trends and problems
S. E. Finer, *The Changing British Party System, 1945–1979* (American Enterprise Institute, 1980), S. H. Beer, *Britain Against Itself* (Faber,

1982) and R. Rose, *Do Parties make a difference?* (expanded 2nd edn., Macmillan, 1984) are stimulating interpretations. Patrick Dunleavy in a chapter entitled 'Analysing British Politics' in H. Drucker, *et al.*, eds., *op. cit.*, examines approaches to British politics in a valuable way.

A number of works can be recommended as particularly useful on developments between the 1950s and 1970s. Peter Self, 'Are we worse governed?' *New Society*, 19 May 1977, lucidly analyses the major trends in British government since the 1950s. The essays by Anthony King, John P. Mackintosh and Samuel Brittan in Anthony King, ed., *Why is Britain becoming harder to govern?* (BBC, 1976) contain many insights into the problems of contemporary governments. W. J. Stankiewicz, ed., *British Government in an Era of Reform* (Collier-Macmillan, 1976), includes 'Parliament and the pressure groups', a good survey written for PEP. Although primarily concerned to recommend issues for research, Wyn Grant, 'Corporatism and pressure groups', and Dennis Kavanagh, 'Party politics in question', in Dennis Kavanagh and Richard Rose, eds, *New Trends in British Politics* (Sage Publication, 1977) have much of value to say on contemporary trends in their respective areas of concern. W. Grant and D. March, 'Tripartism: reality or myth?', *Government and Opposition*, vol. 12, no. 2 (Summer, 1977) is a useful discussion of relations between governments and the major producer groups.

R.Rose, *Problem of Party Government*, chapter 16, contains some interesting remarks on coalition which is also analysed by A. J. Beattie, 'British coalition government revisited', in *Government and Opposition*, vol. 2, no. 1 (October 1966–January 1967). A. J. Beattie examines the nature of the contemporary party system in 'The two-party legend', *Political Quarterly*, vol. 45 (1974).

Chapter 7. Parties, Pressure Groups and Democracy

G. M. Higgins and J. J. Richardson, *Political Participation*, Politics Association Occasional Publication, 3 (1976) provides a succinct survey of the theme. Robert Worcester, 'The hidden activists' *New Society* (1972), reprinted in R. Rose, ed., *Studies in British Politics* (3rd edn, Macmillan, 1976) examines the social composition of political activists. Arthur Cyr, 'Current trends in British politics', *Parliamentary Affairs*, vol. 29, no. 1 (winter, 1976) surveys the growth of minor parties and promotional groups.

The best discussions set participation in a context of democratic theory. Bernard Crick, 'Participation and the future of government' in J. A. G. Griffith, ed., *From Policy to Administration* (Allen & Unwin, 1975); J. R. Lucas, *Democracy and Participation* (Penguin, 1976), and Peter Singer, *Democracy and Disobedience* (Oxford University Press, 1973) are all excellent in this regard.

Index